Beyond Reconciliation
Experiencing *Koinonia* across the Racial Divide

Beyond Reconciliation
Experiencing *Koinonia* across the Racial Divide

Terry Roberts, D.Min.

The Curriculum Companion to
Journey to Koinonia:
An Interracial Small Group Experience

Beyond Reconciliation: Experiencing Koinonia *across the Racial Divide*

"When I first began reading *Beyond Reconciliation*, I must admit my skepticism. In fact, I found myself getting angry, thinking, 'Here we go again with a white person telling me that he knows more about the black experience than I do.' But knowing Terry Roberts like I do, as a neighbor and a spiritual confidante, I wanted to give it a chance. As I continued reading, I was delighted to find this was not a 'know-it-all' book. Rather, it was humble enough to ask the question, 'How do we get across the racial divide so that we can experience true koinonia?' The book is an attempt to help us see eye-to-eye, even though we see through differing lenses."
—**Rev. Mel Tapp,** Minister and next-door-neighbor of the author

"Terry Roberts has, through his research and his own ministry, presented a solution to one of the most pressing problems of our day. Terry's passion for godly reconciliation led him to refine his research into a volume that pastors and lay people can use to build a community of real love and acceptance. His book arrives just in time to provide a way forward for pastors on both sides of the racial divide. The Twenty First Century Church desperately needs this book."
—**Dr. Alan Ehler,** Dean and Professor, Barnett College of Ministry and Theology, Southeastern University, Lakeland, Florida and author of *How to Make Big Decisions Wisely*, Zondervan, 2020

Acknowledgments and Dedication

This book is dedicated to the fourteen individuals—all of them members of Trinity Church—who "traveled" with me on our very first "Journey to *Koinonia*." Their faithful participation and interaction contributed greatly to the success of the "Journey" and validated the concepts contained in this book. LaNae Budden, my capable assistant during the Journey, was one of the fourteen. Always preferring to serve in the background, she committed hours of her time outside of the meetings to administrative details that made the meetings work.

I would also like to thank the congregation of Trinity Church for loving me through this period of my life, when I was doing the research and writing my conclusions, much of which made its way into my Sunday morning sermons. Thank you for your willingness to learn with me and for your patience with me when at times I may have been a little over-zealous in my excitement about the things I was learning.

My wife, Sandra, has been a constant source of encouragement and support for this project. She was by my side throughout the Journey to *Koinonia,* serving the group at every turn. She has continued to encourage me and support me as we endeavor to live out the principles in this book.

Finally, I am honored that Bishop Larry Jackson agreed to write the foreword. He pastors a great church, and he mentors pastors. He is also known for his ministry with *Promise Keepers* and other interracial gatherings of men. Through his insightful messages and our fellowship together, I have been enriched. I am also indebted to Bishop Jackson for the title of this book. A number of years ago, he co-wrote a noteworthy book titled *Beyond Reconciliation,* a book I highly recommend. As I considered what to call my book, I decided to borrow his title, because it clearly and succinctly states my premise. I'm pleased that he is pleased with my decision.

TABLE of CONTENTS

Foreword

It has been a joy developing a friendship with Pastor Terry Roberts and his church family at Trinity church in Columbia, South Carolina. Pastor Roberts has a great passion for the Lord and the advancement of His kingdom. I've spoken for Pastor Roberts several times in addition to speaking at other events held at Trinity.

The subject of reconciliation is very near to my heart. I believe that one of the main reasons the worldwide Church has failed to convince people of Jesus' lordship and greatness is that it fails to function in divine unity.

While discussing this problem with Pastor Roberts over dinner one evening before a scheduled speaking engagement, I learned that he did his doctoral research in this area. He recalled that I had spoken about the recipe for divine unity given to the Church by the Apostle Paul in Galatians 3:27-29: "For as many of you as have been baptized into Christ have put on Christ. There is neither Jew nor Greek, there is neither bond nor free, there is neither male nor female: for ye are all one in Christ Jesus. And if ye be Christ's, then are ye Abraham's seed, and heirs according to the promise."

Paul identifies three areas that must be surrendered to Christ if we are to be one in Christ. We must surrender our culture ("neither Jew nor Greek"), our rights ("neither bond nor free"), and any hint of gender superiority ("neither male nor female"). I will address the first of the three subjects the way I treat it during my speaking engagements. I say, "I'm culturally sensitive but not culturally controlled." I explain that a black man at one time did live in this physical house called a body that

1

I now occupy. But he died, and I was sent from heaven to take his place.

I also reference 2 Corinthians 5:17: "Therefore if any man be in Christ, he is a new creature: old things are passed away; behold, all things are become new." This scripture is taught across the entire landscape of the Church, but it is most often applied to salvation from sin and not to total transformation. The passage ends with "all things are become new." And "all" means all!

During dinner that night we discussed the book you are now reading, and at that time it did not have a title. I co-authored a book while living in Fayetteville, North Carolina, with my friend Michael Fletcher, and we titled it *Beyond Reconciliation*. When Pastor Roberts told of his decision to use the same title, I was very excited.

Never before have we in the Church (as well as those outside the Church) needed to better understand how to move past racial tensions and to walk in true unity. It has been over twenty-nine years since Rodney King uttered those famous words, "Can we all just get along?"

This book addresses the need to get along without becoming clones of each other. It was God's intent and exceptional design to create us all different. Father God has never produced a duplicate of anything, and He especially didn't duplicate cultures. It is our responsibility to learn how to work and walk together while enjoying our differences.

Jacob gave his son Joseph a coat of many colors. Joseph is a typology of Jesus Christ, and the coat he received from his Father is a type of the Body of Christ. Notice, it is one coat with many colors, a macramé, all sewn together in perfect unity.

It is time for the Church to decide to look at the sin of racism and bring healing to a nation in desperate need to be free. Only the Church has this mandate to love their enemies and do good to their neighbors. The Church is called to bridge the gap. Jesus placed His blood on a mercy seat in heaven where two angels stood looking down on the seat. These two angels represent righteousness and justice. The Church, not a political party, has the mandate to demonstrate and function in both of these qualities at the same time.

Beyond Reconciliation will give a blueprint for churches to work both within and beyond their doors to bring diverse communities together. Christians will better understand that we are all one and should do everything in our power to work as one. Jesus said that when we work and function as one, then the world will believe that the Father sent Him, and that He is our Lord. Finally, we will demonstrate true *koinonia*, and the world will see real love and unity. The Church is the only thing in the earth that makes Rodney King's plea a reality.

Bishop Larry Jackson
Bethel Outreach International Church
Charlotte, North Carolina

Introduction

*"Hospitality is a way of life fundamental to Christian identity.
With a profound commitment to racial reconciliation as an expression of the
power of the gospel, we have pushed past the superficial layers of friendliness
to the deeper strata of respect, care, and honesty."* [1]

*"When we take time to be with people, a relationship is developed.
Both parties drop their masks; they respect each other's convictions
and understand each other's sufferings."* [2]

Much has been written about racial reconciliation. So much, in fact, that one more book on the subject might seem a bit redundant. So let me say at the outset, this book is not primarily about reconciliation, although I hope it will help in that noble cause. After all, reconciliation *is* a noble cause and a biblical theme.[3] In fact, we might say that reconciliation—the restoration of broken relationships—is *the* theme of the Bible.

In the Church, however, reconciliation (as in "racial reconciliation") is not enough. Something more is needed. Reconciliation means that all is forgiven, that I don't hate you anymore, that I accept you as a brother or sister in Christ. That's good. But not good enough.

---

[1] Christine Pohl, *Making Room: Recovering Hospitality as a Christian Tradition,* Kindle e–book, locations 22, 24-30.

[2] Michael Pocock and Joseph Henriques, *Cultural Change and Your Church: Helping Your Church Thrive in a Diverse Society* (Grand Rapids, MI: Baker Books, 2002), 158.

[3] For example, see 2 Corinthians 5:14-21.

The concern of this book is that racial reconciliation, wonderful as it is, too often stops short of us becoming real family with the people we reconcile with. In the Church, we must move beyond reconciliation to intentional fellowship with each other across racial lines.

Fellowship. That too is a biblical theme. Biblical fellowship is how the barriers come down. It's how we really get to know each other. It's how we come to love each other in practical, not just theoretical, terms. And that is especially true when it comes to relationships across the racial divide. In their book *Cultural Change and Your Church*, Michael Pocock and Joseph Henriques capture the idea in these words:

> "When we take time to be with people, a relationship is developed. Both parties drop their masks; they respect each other's convictions and understand each other's sufferings. … As we listen to our friend's real beliefs and problems, we divest our minds of the false images we may have harbored, and we are determined also to be real. … We no longer desire to score points or win a victory. We love the person too much to boost our ego at his or her expense."[4]

The Greek word translated "fellowship" in the New Testament is *koinonia,* and in this book, I will use the Greek word a lot, because it means so much more than any single English word.

First and foremost, *koinonia* is vertical. It happens between Jesus and the believer.[5] That is where it begins, but not where it ends. This essential, personal relationship between a believer and his Lord *sources* the horizontal relationship between believer and believer. And, according to 1 John 4:16-21, you can't have one without the other. The vertical and horizontal aspects of *koinonia* are essential to each other.

---

[4] Michael Pocock and Joseph Henriques, *Cultural Change and Your Church: Helping Your Church Thrive in a Diverse Society* (Grand Rapids, MI: Baker Books, 2002), 158.
[5] 1 John 1:3, 7

But when it comes to *koinonia* across racial lines, for some reason there seems to be a disconnect. And that disconnect is why a book like this is needed. In the pages of this book, I invite you to join me on a journey that will explore the nature of interracial *koinonia*—why it is necessary, barriers that hinder it, how it works in actual practice, and how it benefits us when we achieve it.

So, with that as the context, let's briefly define the Greek word.[6] *Koinonia* is the mutual sharing in the life of Jesus that believers should experience in their interpersonal relationships. *Koinonia* expresses a partnership around a common Person (Jesus Christ) and a common cause (His mission in the world). In such a partnership, ethnic and cultural differences no longer divide us.

Genuine *koinonia* will not remain within the four walls of the church. It leaves the sanctuary after worship and goes with the members into the ordinary activities of their lives. Where this does not happen, true, biblical *koinonia* does not exist. To quote a popular—and accurate—definition, "*Koinonia* is doing life together."

The problem is, that kind of fellowship across racial lines isn't happening as much as it should. And when it happens, it is viewed as the anomaly. For example, a recent front-page article in our local newspaper featured the story of two high-profile pastors in our city who have forged a strong friendship with each other. What made the story newsworthy is that one of those pastors is white and the other is black. The article noted this comment by the black pastor: "We know of no other strong, close, sincere … relationship between a white pastor and a black pastor. I'm disheartened because it's unfortunately too rare." The article also quoted a mutual friend of the pastors, who said, "There is still an unfortunate gap in relations between white

---

[6] For a more expansive treatment of the word and the concept, see chapter nine.

Christians and black Christians in America. I don't think it is from …
a desire to stay separate, it's just kind of the way it is."[7]

This is something I've noticed even within our multi-racial church. On
Sundays, our people worship well together across racial lines. But I
don't see a lot of interracial fellowship happening throughout the
week. And I wonder why that is. As a white Christian, I know what
"table time" with African American friends has done for me, and I
want everyone in our church to benefit from it. Nevertheless, it just
doesn't seem to happen as much as it could and should.

A few years ago I took a couple dozen of our church members to a
state-wide church conference. At noon, when the participants broke
for lunch, I went looking for our people in the cafeteria. The
arrangement was open seating, and I wanted to sit with our folks. What
I found surprised and disappointed me. Our white members were
seated together at one table and our black members at another table
nearby. I walked over to the tables, got their attention, and asked,
"What is this? Are we back to the days of segregation?" My question
evoked nervous laughter, but no one answered. I think they were a bit
embarrassed. Good. I wanted to make the point that their seating
arrangement was *not* good. I think they got the point.

This is not to suggest that our people are unloving across racial lines.
On the contrary, Blacks and Whites in our church exhibit wonderful
unity. It's just that I don't see a lot of interracial fellowship going on
outside of church activities. Simply put, our people worship together
on Sunday, but they don't eat together on Monday.

Now, I don't mean to overstate the value of table fellowship or make
it the sum total of what comprises *koinonia*. Table fellowship is only
one of several components of *koinonia*. But, having clarified that, let

---

[7] Lezlie Patterson, "Benedict Degree Honors Friendship of Two Pastors,
One White, One Black," *The State*, Vol. 129, No. 86, Tuesday, May 14, 2019, 5A.

me underscore the point that breaking bread together is an *essential* component of biblical *koinonia*. As Christine Pohl observes in her wonderful book, *Making Room: Recovering Hospitality as a Christian Tradition*, "I learned to cherish potluck dinners where you were never entirely sure what you were eating but it usually tasted good, and the fellowship tasted a bit like the Kingdom. ... [W]e were learning to welcome one another across racial and socioeconomic differences. With a profound commitment to racial reconciliation as an expression of the power of the gospel, we have pushed past the superficial layers of friendliness to the deeper strata of respect, care, and honesty."[8]

So why doesn't it happen more often—across racial lines?

There's probably a natural explanation for that, and it goes something like this: "Birds of a feather flock together." In other words, like attracts like. People tend to hang with people who are like them. One reason for this is that it's just easier. When we're with people like ourselves, we know the culture, we speak the same language, we understand the humor, we like the same food, we share similar political views, or we think we do, anyway. It's just more comfortable, because we don't have to mind our p's and q's so much. We can let our hair down, be ourselves, and if a little ethnic joke slips out, we don't have to worry about someone being offended. (By the way, I'm pleased to say that I can't remember the last time I've heard a member of my race tell an ethnic joke. That spells progress!) Still, it's just more *comfortable* being with people like ourselves.

But, is that what God has called His Church to be? Comfortable? In the previous paragraph, I said that our monocultural fellowship has a *natural* explanation. But, are we content just to be natural? What about being *spiritual*?[9] Because, that is what it takes to develop relationships

---

[8] Pohl, *Making Room: Recovering Hospitality as a Christian Tradition*, Kindle e-book, locations 22, 24-30.

[9] Consider Paul's use of this word in 1 Corinthians 3:1ff.

across racial lines. It takes authentic spirituality. It takes intentionality in pursuing those relationships, stepping out of our comfort zones and doing things that don't come natural. And it probably takes something of the supernatural as well. That's the part God promises to supply—the supernatural—if we're willing to step beyond "what comes natural."

During my doctoral program, when I was asked to select a topic for my dissertation, my mind turned to this concern, and after prayer and consultation with my cohort leaders, I decided to research race relations and explore ways to promote interracial fellowship in a local church.

What you will read in this book is largely the product of that research, though I have repackaged it in a popular style I think you will find enjoyable. Having said that, I hope it will also be appreciated by those who value solid research and careful citation of sources. Most importantly, I hope it will inspire you to pursue *koinonia* with people whose skin color and culture are different from yours. If you do, you will reap the benefits, including spiritual growth, broadened perspectives on life, and wonderful friendships. In short, your life will be richer and the church will be stronger.

You will find that this book is divided into three parts. In Part One, I begin with my own story of how God used interracial *koinonia* to change me and my perceptions about people of other races. I will also talk about God's "New Community," the Church, and a unique but often overlooked purpose for which He placed it on earth. I think you will be surprised and delighted to learn that purpose. Also, I talk about the beauty of diversity and God's holy delight in it. Again, I think you will be amazed to see throughout Scripture how God pushes His people to love and embrace ethnic diversity.

However, if we are to embrace and enjoy diversity as God does, we must understand it. If we are to experience real *koinonia* across racial lines, we must know the nature of our diversity—our differences. That is the subject of Part Two, where we will "peel the onion" on those differences. We will learn that they involve far more than race and skin color. Our differences include culture, history, and politics, and these differences are aggravated by corporate pain, racial insensitivity, and racialization. If you are unfamiliar with the last three terms, we'll peel them back as well. They refer to crucial issues that lie just beneath the surface of everyday life in America, invisible to many.

Part Three contains in-depth studies on two New Testament words, *Koinonia* (chapter 9) and *Proslambano* (chapter 10). Chapter 11 provides details about a six-week, small group experience we have used in our church. On that note, let me recommend the companion book to the book you are holding. Titled *Journey to Koinonia: An Interracial Small Group Experience*, it contains all the facts about our small group experience, along with a facilitator's guide for those who might want to conduct a "Journey to *Koinonia*" in their church or group.

Definitions

Having offered a brief working definition of *koinonia*, let me explain the way I will use a few other key words in this book. Like train cars carrying freight, words carry meaning, and that makes them important. Problem is, words can mean different things to different people. So, here's what I intend by the following words:

Diversity. For the purpose of this book, I will restrict the meaning of this term to racial, cultural, and political differences.

Race. Modern science rejects the notion of multiple races within the human species, validating Paul's statement in Acts 17:26: "From one man [God] made every nation of men." In other words, there is only one race—the human race. Personally, I prefer the term "ethnicity" when referring to the observable physical distinctions within the human family (what we often call "race"). However, because the term "race" is so widely used in our everyday vernacular, and since it often conveys the idea of "ethnicity," I will use both terms interchangeably.

Racial Designations. Some prefer the term "African American," others prefer the term "black." Such preferences are typically associated with one's generation or geographic region of the country. For simplicity, I will use the terms interchangeably. The term "white" generally refers to non-Hispanic white people.

Political Designations. The word "conservative" can mean "disposed to preserve existing conditions, institutions, etc., or to restore traditional ones, and to limit change."[10] The terms "liberal" and "progressive" can be defined as "favorable to progress or reform, as in political or religious affairs; … pertaining to a political party advocating measures of progressive political reform."[11] Although these terms are often used as unflattering labels we smear on one another, I do not intend them that way. In the chapter on politics, for the sake of simplicity, I apply the term "conservative" to people who tend to vote Republican and the term "liberal" to people who tend to vote Democratic in national elections. Admittedly, these two terms are less than adequate, and they can even be misleading, because the same individual can hold liberal sentiments about certain issues and conservative leanings about others, as we shall see.

Evangelicals. I use this word to refer to protestant, Bible-believing Christians, as a way to distinguish them from certain mainline denominations that do not accept the inerrancy and authority of Scripture. Evangelicals are frequently associated with conservative politics (especially in the South), but they are by no means monolithic in that regard. A number of Evangelical denominations, including the Southern Baptists and the Assemblies of God, have publicly repented

---

[10] "Conservative," in *Random House Webster's Unabridged Dictionary*, 2nd ed. (New York: Random House, 1997), 433.
[11] "Liberal," in *Random House Webster's Unabridged Dictionary*, 2nd ed. (New York: Random House, 1997), 1108.

for past racist policies, renounced racism in all its forms, and elected people of color to their highest offices. Today, forty percent of Assemblies of God church members in the U.S. are people of color, who also comprise its fastest-growing block.

A Disclaimer: I am a white man. That means I view things through "white lenses." In the following pages, I attempt to take those lenses off at times and put on "black lenses." With either set of lenses, I don't have 20/20 vision. If you see distortions in the following pages, or if my observations evoke questions, do me this favor: Write and tell me. I welcome your thoughts. You will find my email address on the publication page at the beginning of this book.

That being said, come along with me on this journey. I think you'll enjoy it. I know you'll be better informed about vital issues of our times. Most importantly, I hope and pray you'll be changed for the better by what you discover along the way!

Dr. Terry Roberts
Trinity Church
Columbia, South Carolina

Part One
God's Eternal Plan ~
Beloved Community

God's purpose in all this was to use the church to display his wisdom in its rich variety to all the unseen rulers and authorities in the heavenly places. This was his eternal plan, which he carried out through Christ Jesus our Lord.
Ephesians 3:10,11 NLT

1

THE POWER OF *KOINONIA*

Dialogue opens windows into our lives so others can understand our life journey.
With that in mind, I want to open a window into my journey
from racism to reconciliation and beyond.
Prepare yourself. What you are about to read is gut-level honest.

To this day, I remember how strange it seemed, seeing black hands holding our tableware and black lips drinking from our glass.

The year was 1974, and I was a 25-year-old pastor serving an inner-city mission church in New Orleans.

Janice had recently come to faith in Christ at a sidewalk service in front of our church. She had an incredible story. She had served time for killing her abusive husband and had just been released from prison. When we gave the invitation to receive Christ, she stepped out of the little crowd and knelt in prayer on the sidewalk. She began attending our church and growing in her Christian walk. Now, she was sitting at our kitchen table.

It isn't Janice's story that rivets her in my mind. During the year that Sandra and I served that church, we met several others with similar, heart-wrenching stories. I think the reason that table experience with Janice remains indelible in my memory, is that she was the first black person we had ever invited to eat with us in our home. In order for you to understand why that was such a big deal for us, you will need to know something about our lives prior to that moment. As I tell you the story, understand that I'm not proud of it. In fact, what I am about to share prompts a sadness in me that we could have been so blind.

You see, Sandra and I were both raised in the Deep South during the Jim Crow era. We attended segregated schools, and we lived in segregated neighborhoods. We worshiped in a segregated church. In one town we lived in, the doctors' offices had separate waiting rooms for Whites and Blacks (although the treatment areas were the same!). We ate in restaurants where only white people ate.

The idea of sitting down and eating with black people was totally foreign to us, something we would never have considered. It just wasn't done.

Now don't get me wrong. We weren't "uppity." My family was lower middle class. Daddy was a minimum-wage laborer and Mama was a secretary. So, even with two incomes, money was always tight. Our house had "central heat"—a kerosene stove in the center of the house that we huddled around on cold mornings. When we finally got air conditioning, it was a window unit in our dining room. I know what it feels like to live on "the other side of the tracks."

Furthermore, we were taught never to mistreat anyone because of their race. After all, we were Christians. We loved the Lord, and we knew that He loved everyone regardless of their race. We knew that, because we sang it every week in Sunday School:

> "Jesus loves the little children,
> All the children of the world,
> Red and yellow, black and white,
> They are precious in his sight,
> Jesus loves the little children of the world."

Since Jesus loved all the little children—even the red, yellow, and black ones—we had to love them, too, of course.

Nevertheless, by spoken and unspoken prompts from our culture—as well as our parents and our pastors—we came to believe that black people were beneath us on the social ladder, and interaction with them was on an as-needed basis only. Socializing with them wasn't on our radar.

We took for granted the public "rules" that went with our segregated society, including two water fountains and two sets of bathrooms—one for "White" and the other for "Colored." Of course, we lived in a big city where dual accommodations were common. What I didn't know at the time was that in rural areas and smaller towns, accommodations for "Colored" didn't exist. I didn't know that black mothers would say to their children, "Today, we're going to town. So go use the bathroom and get a drink of water, because when we get to town, there won't be any place for you to do that."

If you are under the age of fifty, you probably can't imagine how we could see things as we did. But, that's the thing about culture. The people within a culture never see their own culture. Our culture serves as an "invisible veil," blinding us to the wrongness of our attitudes and behaviors. To those within the culture, this is just the way things are. That's why I don't resent my parents or my pastors for what they transmitted to me. They were simply passing on what had been passed to them. No one questioned it. True, a few people here and there were ahead of their times, but most of us were simply products of our times.

Of course, people on the outside of a culture can see clearly what's wrong with that culture, because it's different from what they are used to. But the ones on the inside can't see it. That's why, if we're painfully honest, none of us is truly objective. We all see life through the lenses we were given, and few of us question what we see—or don't see. That's why we couldn't see racism. We might never have seen it, had something not come along that forced us to see the invisible.

When the name Martin Luther King, Jr. first came to my attention, I was a teenager. That's when things began to change about the way I saw—or didn't see—my culture. At the time, all we knew about King was what we saw on the news, and most often, that was unsettling. We saw the mass protests and marches coordinated by King and his followers, often an undulating sea of black, pushing its way toward our white shoreline, and it scared us. We wondered why these people were so upset, why they wanted to cause all this trouble, why they couldn't just settle down and accept life as it was. And we worried about how it would all end.

We also saw water cannons and police dogs and billy clubs. Though such measures made us uncomfortable, we didn't complain, because, to our minds, these people were upsetting the apple cart, and such measures were necessary to maintain "law and order."

With the passing of time, things changed in the South. The civil rights movement brought about the integration of schools, neighborhoods, and the market place. Eventually, interaction between Whites and Blacks began to normalize, at least to some extent.

As I matured spiritually, and as I gained some life experience, my perceptions about race began to change. Little by little, I began to encounter black people in *my* settings. A black student enrolled in our otherwise all-white Bible college, and he seemed nice. I liked him. In New Orleans, we met and befriended Janice, our African American dinner guest. We came to really love Janice like a member of our family. And so, for others we met there.

One week, our New Orleans church hosted a guest speaker who was African American. His name was Bob Harrison, and he held the distinction of being the first black minister ordained by our denomination. Bob was a gifted speaker, musician, and author, and I admired the way God used him in ministry. I also enjoyed fellowshipping with him at a coffee shop in the French Quarter. That's another table experience I'll never forget.

Bob's ordination with our denomination hadn't come quickly or easily. For years his applications were denied, again and again, because denominational policy prohibited the ordination of black ministers. Only after Bob was tapped by the Billy Graham organization to serve as an associate evangelist, did our denominational officials wake up and smell the coffee. Bob graciously accepted their overdue invitation to be ordained, but the experience, along with other slights and injustices, had left their residue of hurt. Some of that spilled out in our conversation, and some of it I read in Bob's book.[1] I think that was my first encounter with the cruelty of racism. Suddenly, it was up close and personal. It was hurting somebody I knew, someone I considered a friend.

During one conversation, Bob and I talked about Martin Luther King, Jr., and I got Bob's "inside" perspective about the man, which gave me a better impression of King than I had previously entertained. Then the conversation turned to politics. I asked Bob if he was a conservative. I was sure he was, because I assumed all true Christians were conservative, and I knew Bob was a true Christian. Bob's answer both surprised and instructed me. He said, "When you consider the injustices my people have endured for centuries, why would I want to *conserve* the status quo?" Bob's answer didn't radically alter my political leanings, but it sure opened a window that helped me understand his.

My brief friendship with Bob Harrison whetted my appetite for friendships with other black ministers. I began to participate in interracial ministerial associations. At one point, I was befriended by a young black pastor, and we often looked to each other for spiritual encouragement. Despite our ethnic and cultural differences, we

---

[1] Bob Harrison and James Montgomery, *When God Was Black* (Grand Rapids, MI: Zondervan, 1971).

discovered that we shared similar challenges and concerns. This happened before *Promise Keepers* came along to encourage such interracial fellowship.

In my city of Columbia, South Carolina, I joined an interracial group of pastors who came together weekly specifically for the purpose of prayer. For some reason, our numbers quickly dwindled to no more than five or six, most of them black. Leadership of the group fell to an older black pastor, whom I came to love as a father. That little gathering continued for five years, until the leader felt it had accomplished its purpose. We met on the twenty-fifth floor of the tallest building in our state. Our meeting room overlooked the state capitol building, which prompted us to pray for government leaders and matters of public policy.

Many times, we ate together after our prayer time. Our conversations around the table often followed our prayer topics, and they were candid. We shared our honest opinions, and we often disagreed. But, we always disagreed respectfully, and we never allowed disagreements to affect our fellowship in Christ. If anything, those honest disagreements strengthened our fellowship, because we never felt the need to tiptoe around delicate matters for fear of offending one another. Everybody knew where everybody stood on the issues, and we were okay with that.

Fellowship with my black minister friends exposed me to their life experiences, and those experiences gave me insight into their viewpoints. I didn't always agree with their viewpoints, but I came to understand *why* they saw things as they did. As I attempted to view issues through the lenses of their life journeys, a lot of things began to come clear. I saw and understood things I had never considered. For example, on one occasion, a member of our group was talking about the fear many black men have of being falsely accused. I'll never forget his candid revelation: "Every black man knows the fear of getting onto an elevator where the only other person is a white woman, and you pray that when you get to your floor, she doesn't accuse you of something." That statement opened a window into the inner world of my black friends and gave me a perspective I would never have had without that interracial table time. Such experiences made me keenly aware of the value of fellowship across racial lines.

As the years rolled by, Sandra and I befriended other black people and were befriended by them. We enjoyed fellowshipping with them in our home and theirs, breaking bread, laughing, praying, weeping, agreeing, disagreeing, doing life with them. Some of them were neighbors. Some were members and leaders in the churches we served. We dedicated their babies and later, officiated at the weddings of those "babies," and then dedicated the babies' babies. We officiated at their funerals. We cried with their families. In short, we did life together.

Let me share one more example of how interracial *koinonia* changed me. In June of 2012, the Supreme Court announced its decision on an important issue with strong political implications. I was keenly interested in this case, and when I heard the outcome, I was deeply disappointed and angry.

Coincidentally, on the same day, I needed to make a pastoral visit to the home of one of our black members whose mother had died. On the way to her home, my wife and I discussed the Supreme Court decision, and the more we talked, the angrier I felt. By the time we arrived at our member's home, I had no desire to comfort a family who, due to their political alliances, were probably rejoicing over what I perceived as a major defeat. Nevertheless, determined to fulfill our pastoral duty, we prayed that God would help us comfort this family despite my angry feelings.

As we entered the home, our member introduced us to her siblings, and we managed a pleasant conversation. Near the end of the visit, I asked if we could pray with them, and we all stood and joined hands. As I began to pray, I was startled and humbled as I sensed the presence of Jesus come into that living room. Though I couldn't see Him, I knew He was standing in the middle of that circle. I could tell the others sensed it too by the way they expressed their petitions and thanksgivings. As we prayed "in the Spirit" (Eph. 6:18), it seemed that our hearts melted into one symphony of praise and love to the One at the center of our focus. When the prayer ended, I felt a palpable love, not only for Jesus, but for every person in that room. The issue in my mind that stood between us as a "dividing wall of hostility," melted away in our mutual love and adoration of the One who "is our peace, who has made the two one and has destroyed the barrier" (Eph. 2:14). He was all that mattered, and because He loved us, we loved each other (John 13:34).

The difference in Sandra and me now, compared to where we were in 1974, is remarkable. It's not that we're now "color-blind," as many people say they are. I'm not sure we should be color-blind. I don't think God is. He loves color, and He made lots of it. I think the better way to say it is that, although we see color, we don't recoil from it. We celebrate it. We like the richness it brings to our lives. We appreciate the diversity it brings to our church. Simply put, it's the spice of life. After all, who likes bland food with no seasoning? Who would want a world without color? Who would bother to go to Baskin Robbins if they had only vanilla?

Reflecting back on a lifetime of experiences, some of which I've just shared, it seems to me that what made the difference in our attitude toward people different from ourselves, is fellowship with them: Sitting down together, face to face, often over food, listening to their stories, telling them ours, talking candidly, understanding their struggles, agreeing, disagreeing, laughing, praying,—and loving.

Now, when I sit across the table from a black friend, I no longer need an internal conversation with myself like I did in 1974. I feel totally at ease, totally natural. To quote an old song, "I've grown accustomed to your face." In fact, I can't imagine—don't want to imagine—a world in which the only faces I see at my kitchen table are the same color as mine.

Which, once again, points up the premise of this book: In the Church, reconciliation, great as it is, is not enough. We must move beyond reconciliation to real, intentional fellowship with each other across racial lines. That's how the barriers come down. That's how we really get to know each other. That's how we come to love each other.

But that's not just my experience. That's Bible.

With that in mind, I think it wise to pause and reflect on the biblical reasons for interracial fellowship. As a Bible-believing Christian, that's my starting point. I hope it's yours, too. Either way, I think you'll find the next couple of chapters interesting and informative.

2

GOD'S NEW COMMUNITY

For Christ himself has brought peace to us. He united Jews and Gentiles into one people when, in his own body on the cross, he broke down the wall of hostility that separated us. ... God's purpose in all this was to use the church to display his wisdom in its rich variety to all the unseen rulers and authorities in the heavenly places. This was his eternal plan, which he carried out through Christ Jesus our Lord. Ephesians 2:14; 3:10,11 NLT

Check out any Bible commentary on Ephesians, and you will discover that the theme of this letter by the Apostle Paul is the Church. One of Paul's major points about the Church is God's intention to unite different kinds of people—previously divided by race, culture, or nationality—into one redeemed and unified people, and *to use them to reflect His purpose for all mankind.*

Divided City ~ Divided Church

Paul wrote Ephesians during his house arrest in the city of Rome. By ancient standards, Rome was a mega-tropolis. The cross-roads of the world, Rome was the "New York City" of its day. Its nearly one million residents were a jumble of ethnicities, languages, and cultures. The social distance between those groups was enormous, and the friction was volatile. Homegrown Romans in general disliked immigrants because, to their minds, immigrants had turned Rome into "the dumping-place of the whole world, and there was no vice, no corruption, no ill practice that these foreign crowds had not imported with them."[1] Romans disliked Jews, in particular, because of their strange food customs, holy days, circumcision, and not least, for their success at converting Roman women.[2] To say the least, first-century Rome was a cauldron of ethnic tension, a situation not unlike many cities in America today.

Unfortunately, the church in Rome reflected the social problems of the broader culture around it, a situation too often true of the church everywhere. When you think of the church in Rome, don't picture a huge building where all the Christians came together for worship. No, the church in Rome was a loose network of house churches divided along ethnic and cultural lines. Believing Gentiles met in their various gathering places; Messianic Jews met in their homes and synagogues; and never the twain did meet! And for good reason.

The culture of Jewish believers in the first century was very different from that of Gentile believers. Even their religious practices were different. Although they worshiped the same Lord and followed the same faith (Eph. 4:5), the ways in which they worshiped that "one Lord" and practiced that "one faith" were very different.

According to theologian John Stott, "It is difficult for us to grasp the impassable gulf which yawned in those days between the Jews on the one hand and the Gentiles ... on the other."[3] Observant Jews would not venture into the home of a Gentile for fear of contamination.[4] And Gentiles viewed Jewish practices as just plain weird. The most telling symbol of this ethnic, cultural, and religious division stood—of all places—in the courtyard of the Jewish Temple. That symbol of division was a literal wall that divided Jewish worshipers from Gentile

---

[1] George La Piana, "Foreign Groups in Rome during the First Centuries of the Empire," *Harvard Theological Review* 20, no. 4 (1927): 228.

[2] Craig S. Keener, *Romans: A New Covenant Commentary* (Eugene, OR: Cascade Books, 2009), 160.

[3] John Stott, *The Spirit, the Church, and the World: The Message of Acts*, rev. ed. (Downers Grove, IL: InterVarsity Press, 1990), 185.

[4] See Acts 10:28

worshipers. And the wall had signs posted on it threatening death to any Gentile who ventured beyond it![5]

This was the cultural and religious context into which the Church was born, a context of division and hostility. And that division and hostility quickly infected the young Church. In general, Gentile believers criticized their Jewish brothers and sisters as too legalistic, and Jewish believers questioned whether Gentile believers were even saved.[6] And both groups allowed those differences to divide them into segregated churches.

A Clear Purpose

From within that cultural divide, Paul wrote Ephesians, and against that backdrop of division and hostility, Paul explained one of God's primary purposes for the Church. We know from other Scriptures that the Church is Christ's representative in this world, reflecting His holy character and love to fallen humanity.[7] The Church is also the frontline of Kingdom advancement in the world, the missionary force commissioned to "make disciples of all nations."[8] These well-known purposes of the Church are often expounded from pulpits and framed in mission statements. But to these purposes, Paul adds a further purpose for the Church:

> *God's purpose in all this was to use the church to display his wisdom in its rich variety to all the unseen rulers and authorities in the heavenly places. This was his eternal plan, which he carried out through Christ Jesus our Lord (Ephesians 3:10,11 NLT).*

---

[5] In Ephesians 2:14, Paul refers to this wall as the "dividing wall of hostility." Archeologists have discovered ancient examples of the threatening signs that were posted on the dividing wall.

[6] The "strong" vs. "weak" controversy Paul addresses in Romans 14:1-15:7 probably reflects these tensions between Jewish and Gentile believers.

[7] 1 John 4:17 says, "As He is, so are we in this world."

[8] Matthew 28:19

If you look more closely at that purpose statement, I think you will see three basic ideas:

1) God's purpose was to use the church to display His wisdom in its rich variety
2) To all the unseen rulers and authorities in the heavenly places
3) This was his eternal plan, which he carried out through Christ Jesus our Lord

Let's drill a little deeper into each of those ideas:

1) The Church Displays the Rich Variety of God's Wisdom

Think about that statement: God uses the church to display His wisdom in its rich variety. What is Paul saying?

The words "rich variety" ("manifold" in the KJV) translate the Greek word *polypoikolos*. Say that out loud, slowly: poly-poi-kolos. Used only once in the Bible, this word is a combination of three words: *poly*, which means "many;" *poi*, a contraction of poly; and *kolos*, which means "colors" (you can actually see the English word in the Greek word). So, *poly-poi-kolos* literally means "many, many colored."

In ancient times, Greeks used this word to describe a bouquet of multi-colored flowers. Looking at the bouquet and admiring the creativity of the florist, the ancient Greek would say, "*polypoikolos!*" The word was also used to describe a tapestry with its differing hues and textures of thread woven together to create a picture of some kind. (I have seen such a tapestry that portrays the scene of Jesus blessing the children.) The Greeks would look at the tapestry and, admiring the creativity of the artist, they would say, "*polypoikolos!*"

Remarkably, Paul applies the word to the Church. He says that the "unseen rulers in the heavenly places" look at the Church, and they say, "*polypoikolos!*" They have to acknowledge the creative artistry (wisdom) of God. Why? Because, in the Church, God has brought together people from multiple cultures, different races, various skin-colors, and differing languages—people who were previously divided and hostile to each other—and He has woven them together in such a way that they display a beautiful, cohesive picture of His Son!

Now, to the second idea in Ephesians 3:10:

2) To the Unseen Rulers and Authorities in the Heavenly Places

Who are these "unseen rulers and authorities in the heavenly places?" To answer that, let's look first at the phrase "in the heavenly places." This simply means the spiritual realm, so don't think of it as Heaven proper, where we go to be with the Lord when we die. No, Paul is simply reminding us that there is a spiritual dimension of reality that is unseen to the human eye. It is the realm occupied by angels and demons, and they are the "unseen rulers and authorities." Paul mentions these unseen forces again in Ephesians chapter 6, explaining that our battle is spiritual in nature. We don't fight with people, but with "evil rulers and authorities of the unseen world, against mighty powers in this dark world, and against evil spirits in the heavenly places" (Eph. 6:12 NLT).

To me, that begs the question: Why would God want to display His wisdom to angels and demons?

For one thing, Paul is saying that angels stand in rapturous awe before God's wisdom on display in a unified Church comprising people of every color and culture. Having seen for centuries the devastating division among human beings caused by sin, angels rejoice to see God's plan of human restoration unfolding through His Church!

But Paul also says that Satan and his demons see God's wisdom on display in the Church. Why would God want to display his wisdom to demons?

Remember that Satan hates humankind, because we are the crowning touch of God's creative work and the object of His infinite love. Satan's strategy against humanity is simple: Divide & Destroy. Satan and his hordes of demons work at using national, ethnic, and cultural differences to divide humanity, to segregate us, to make us suspicious and fearful of one another. And fear is the root of prejudice.

Satan's strategy has succeeded. Humanity is divided, Whites against Blacks, Arabs against Jews, Russians against Ukrainians, and so on. As evidence of that division, violence is in our news every week, as one group tries to destroy another. Viewing the mass murder of innocent people again and again, who can seriously question the demonic nature of the division that spawns that murder?

Think of Paul's words again in light of this demonic division in humanity. Paul is saying that, in spite of Satan's effort to divide and destroy human beings, God is up to something that will ultimately foil all of Satan's divisive schemes! And what God is up to involves the Church. Theologian Timothy Gombis says it well:

> The powers have ordered the present evil age in such a way as to exacerbate the divisions within humanity. ... God confounds the powers, however, by creating in Christ one unified, multi-racial body consisting of formerly divided groups of people. And it is the existence of the church as a body set within the hostile environment of the present evil age that proclaims to them the wisdom of God.[9]

Did you see that? God is using the Church to confound the principalities and powers—to frustrate their strategy and impede their efforts to divide and destroy!

Of course, the Church displays God's transforming, inclusive love not only to angels and demons, but also to people. Believers' fervent love for each other, in spite of our differences, stands in stark contrast to the selfish, shattered relationships of this world. That difference

---

[9] Gombis, "Ephesians 3:2-13," 322.

announces hope to a divided world and attracts the hated and the hateful to the joyous fellowship of the Church.

And now, that third idea from Ephesians 3:10:

3) This Was His Eternal Plan, Which He Carried Out through Christ Jesus our Lord

Simply put, God's eternal plan is to unite a fractured human race and to use the Church to display what that will look like. And God is accomplishing it all through His Son, Jesus Christ. In Christ, our differences no longer divide us, as Paul so eloquently states in Ephesians 2:14-16:

> *For Christ himself has brought peace to us. He united Jews and Gentiles into one people when, in his own body on the cross, he broke down the wall of hostility that separated us. ... He made peace between Jews and Gentiles by creating in himself one new people from the two groups. Together as one body, Christ reconciled both groups to God by means of his death on the cross, and our hostility toward each other was put to death.[10]*

Through Christ, God made one new composite body out of two hostile groups—Jews and Gentiles. Through His death, Jesus has put to death the enmity that separated Jews and Gentiles, and He has made them "one new people." Jesus gave that new people a name. He called them "my church," and He promised that even the gates of Hell would not prevail against His purpose for them![11] If Jesus can unite Jews and Gentiles into one Church, He can certainly unite black and white Christians. For this reason, the Church is God's "new community" in the world. Indeed, it is an entirely new *kind* of community, where our differences no longer divide us.

This is not to minimize our differences. As we will see in the coming chapters, our differences are very real, and they involve far more than

---

[10] New Living Translation
[11] Matthew 16:18

race and skin color. They involve culture and tradition, which is expressed in our worship preferences, the way we conduct our services and the way we dress for church, what time we arrive for church and how long we stay there, to name just a few. Our differences also involve our histories. Although African Americans and white Americans share the same national history, their *experience* with that history is very different. Our differences also involve politics, which Alice Patterson calls the "Grand Canyon" of racial division in America.[12]

The key to achieving unity and *koinonia* across racial lines is not to deny or side-step our differences. The key is to embrace their reality while submitting them to a greater Reality. And here's the greater Realty: Despite our differences, we have a common denominator that brings us together and makes us one, and that common denominator is our mutual love for Jesus Christ. Let me say it this way: Even though your skin color is different from mine, I love you, and the reason I love you is that I love Jesus and I love everyone He loves!

This may be what Martin Luther King, Jr. had in mind when he coined the term "beloved community."[13] The Church is beloved of God and beloved of those who are in it. King knew that if Jesus could unite Jews and Gentiles, He can unite black people and white people, and for that matter, people of any ethnicity and cultural background, and make them one body in Him. King knew that our mutual love for the One who loved us and gave Himself for us is a powerful adhesive that holds us together. As I behold Jesus in you, I love Him and I love the unique expression of Him that comes to me through you.

We in the body of Christ have another common denominator. We are indwelt by the same Holy Spirit. The apostle Paul is emphatic about this in Ephesians 4:4: "There is one body and one Spirit," and

---

[12] Alice Patterson, *Bridging the Racial and Political Divide: How Godly Politics Can Transform a Nation* (San Jose, CA: Transformational Publications, 2010), 23.

[13] Marsh, *The Beloved Community*, location 144.

therefore, he urges us to be "diligent to preserve the unity of the Spirit in the bond of peace."[14] One mark of the Spirit's presence and work in any believer is the pull toward other believers—especially toward believers different from ourselves. That pull is not natural. It is supernatural.

God's purpose for the Church will prevail!

Let me tell you about a fascinating discovery made by a professor at the University of North Texas. In his study of interracial relationships, George Yancey wanted to determine what kinds of settings tended to promote racial harmony. He wondered if people of different races who worked together or studied together or lived in the same neighborhood, found it easier to overcome racial biases simply through their association with each other in those settings.

Using data from the 1990 General Social Science Survey, Yancy learned that something called "contact hypothesis," which was often touted as the key to racial harmony, simply doesn't work. Contact hypothesis is the idea that simply bringing people together across racial lines will produce more harmonious relations. For example, if people of different ethnicities work together on the same job or live together in the same neighborhood, they will develop better relationships. However, Yancey's research suggested that simply wasn't true. Integration in those settings failed to heal racial tensions.

Remarkably, Yancey discovered one setting that does improve racial relations: The Church! According to Yancey's study, people who worship and fellowship together in integrated churches "engage in less stereotyping and have lower levels of social distance" toward each other.

In other words, God is using the Church to do exactly what He intended. He is using the Church to bring people together in loving

---

[14] New American Standard Version

relationships across racial lines. God is using the Church to show a divided humanity that something better is possible and is coming. God is using the Church to show the devil that his plan to divide and destroy humanity will ultimately fail! Let's read Ephesians 3:10,11 again with that in mind:

> God's purpose in all this was to use the church to display his wisdom in its rich variety to all the unseen rulers and authorities in the heavenly places. This was his eternal plan, which he carried out through Christ Jesus our Lord.

Regrettably, at the present time, the church in America has a lot of ground to cover in that regard, because the church has been among the slowest groups to integrate, lagging behind the corporate world, academia, and the military. As King famously observed: "I am ashamed and appalled that in America, Eleven o'clock on Sunday mornings is still the most segregated hour of the week."[15] King made that statement in a sermon in 1953. Current studies suggest that not much has changed since then. Today, ninety-three percent of churches in America remain mono-cultural.[16] George Yancey (of the Yancey Study just cited) laments, "The dearth of interracial churches within American society undoubtedly reflects the continuing and persistent racial gap."

The good news is that, however slowly, the complexion of the American church is changing. Studies show that from 1998 to 2007, the percentage of Evangelical mega-churches that are multi-ethnic has risen from 6 to 25 percent! Clearly, God is up to something and His

---

[15] Martin Luther King, Jr., *Advocate of the Social Gospel, September 1948 - March 1963*, vol. 6, The Papers of Martin Luther King, Jr (Berkeley: University of California Press, 2007), 149. (King preached this sermon, titled "Communism's Challenge to Christianity," on August 9, 1953, while serving as his father's associate pastor at Ebenezer Baptist Church in Atlanta.)

[16] Curtiss Paul DeYoung, "Shaping Congregations for Faithfulness across Divides" (Lecture presented at the Summer Institute, Duke University Center for Reconciliation, June 1, 2012). DeYoung defines a multi-ethnic church as one with no more than 80% of the congregation from the same culture.

intention for His church, as expressed in Ephesians 3:10,11, will prevail. Allow me to quote theologian Timothy Gombis again:

> The powers have ordered the present evil age in such a way as to exacerbate the divisions within humanity. ... God confounds the powers, however, by creating in Christ one unified, multi-racial body consisting of formerly divided groups of people. And it is the existence of the church as a body set within the hostile environment of the present evil age that proclaims to them the wisdom of God.[17]

"The Great Commission of the Old Testament"

One "unified, multi-racial body" has always been central to God's plan. It didn't begin with Paul's words to the Ephesians or even with Jesus' issuing of the Great Commission in the Gospels. Go all the way back to Genesis, to His call and commissioning of Abraham and you see it: "In you all the families of the earth will be blessed" (Gen. 12:3). Christopher Wright calls this the "Great Commission of the Old Testament."[18] God has always planned to bring together people of "every nation and tribe" and unite them in His Son. That, according to Paul, is God's eternal purpose which He carried out in Christ. Paul states this in the past tense as if it has already been accomplished. In fact, the ultimate triumph of God's purpose for the church is so sure, so certain, that Jesus showed the apostle John a breathtaking "revelation" of what it will look like when it is actually accomplished:

> *After this I saw a vast crowd, too great to count, from every nation and tribe and people and language, standing in front of the throne and before the Lamb. They were clothed in white robes and held palm branches in their hands. And they were shouting with a mighty shout, "Salvation comes from our God who sits on the throne and from the Lamb!" (Rev. 7:9-10 NLT)*

---

[17] Gombis, "Ephesians 3:2-13," 322.

[18] Christopher J. H. Wright, *The Mission of God's People: A Biblical Theology of the Church's Mission* (Grand Rapids, MI: Zondervan, 2010), 71.

John concludes this vision of a multi-racial body of believers with the promise of ultimate justice for all who have felt the iron heel of man's oppression:

> *They will never again be hungry or thirsty; they will never be scorched by the heat of the sun. For the Lamb on the throne will be their Shepherd. He will lead them to springs of life-giving water. And God will wipe every tear from their eyes." (Rev. 7:16-17 NLT)*

In other words, when that vision of a unified Church becomes reality, every injustice will be made right. All suffering will be relieved. All division will be healed!

Not that we should just sit around and wait for God to do it all. We are to work for justice in our present broken world. But, we must not wait until we achieve justice to begin preserving the unity of the Spirit in the bond of peace.[19] Neither should we wait until we all see eye to eye on every issue. We must accept the fact that members of the redeemed community—white and black—often carry the residue of their own brokenness. Remarkably, God still uses the redeemed community, with its brokenness, to heal and restore the broken. In the words of Tim Chester,

> The Christian community is both a sign and a promise of God's coming liberation. ... We are the presence of God's liberating kingdom in a broken world. ... We are to welcome the broken people to a community of broken people. We are the community among whom liberation is a present reality—the jubilee people who live with new economic and social relationships. We are the light of the world, a city on a hill.[20]

With all its challenges, diversity is beautiful. God certainly thinks so. He designed it into the universe, and intended it for the human family

---

[19] New American Standard Version
[20] Tim Chester, *Good News to the Poor: Social Involvement and the Gospel* (Wheaton, IL: Crossway, 2013), Kindle e–book, Locations 1660–1675.

and for His Church. Let's pause and reflect on the beauty of our diversity. Let's admire the artistry of our Creator and appreciate His intentionality in making a world characterized by almost infinite variety. That's the topic of the next chapter.

3
THE BEAUTY OF DIVERSITY
And the Nature of the New Community

God has planned since the beginning of time to cultivate diversity among human beings. When people tried to circumvent His plan, God intervened by creating many languages. Distinctions would have developed naturally over time, and changes would undoubtedly have taken place anyway if the people had spread out and obeyed God. His intervention [at Babel] merely sped up the process of developing the various ethnic groups that brought about His intended diversity.[1]

Here's a paradox for you: A big enemy of unity is the demand for uniformity. Uniformity is the insistence that members of a community adhere to one culture, come from one ethnicity, appreciate one style of worship, and so on. In other words, that they walk in lock-step with each other, often under the control of some intimidating personality.

God is not into uniformity. Scripture clearly shows that God delights in diversity, both in the created order—the cosmos—and in the new creation—the Church.

Diversity in the Cosmos

And God said, "Let the water teem with living creatures, and let birds fly above the earth across the expanse of the sky." So God created the great creatures of the sea and every living and moving thing with which the water teems, according to their kinds, and every winged bird according to its kind.

---

[1] Randy Woodley, *Living in Color: Embracing God's Passion for Ethnic Diversity* (Downers Grove, IL: IVP Books, 2004), 22. Kindle ed., location 21.

And God saw that it was good…. And God said, "Let the land produce living creatures according to their kinds" (Gen. 1:20-24).

This passage from Genesis and a simple observation of nature lead to the unavoidable conclusion that God likes diversity. He not only created birds, sea creatures, and land animals with their obvious differences, He created almost infinite varieties within each of these classifications, a fact suggested by the phrase "according to their kinds" (Gen. 1:24).

Randy Woodley describes how God programmed into creation

> innovation and extravagance, diversity and lavishness. God is the artist who formed the planet Saturn and its beautiful surrounding rings. He is the humorist who formed the giraffe and the narwhale, the armadillo and the platypus. God is the designer who set the constellations in place, who causes roses to bloom and who enables bees to make honey. We are not threatened by the stars that tower overhead or by a blooming rose or by the taste of honey in our tea. Should we be so surprised or threatened to find that God also created such diversity in human beings—all distinct and all equal—or that He insists that every culture be unique in its own right?[2]

Diversity in the Human Race

In the passage quoted above, Woodley mentions the crowning achievement of creation—humankind—as a further study in diversity.

Hold that thought. Before discussing diversity within the human family, let me state emphatically that there is only one race—the human race. Modern science has confirmed this, demonstrating conclusively that no fundamental biological differences exist within the human family.[3] And long before modern science came to that

---

[2] Randy Woodley, *Living in Color: Embracing God's Passion for Ethnic Diversity* (Downers Grove, IL: IVP Books, 2004), 22. Kindle ed., location 163.

[3] Philip F. Esler, *Conflict and Identity in Romans: The Social Setting of Paul's Letter* (Minneapolis, MN: Fortress Press, 2003), 52. This fact is addressed briefly in

conclusion, the Apostle Paul stated it when he preached to the people at Athens: "From one man [God] made every nation of men (Acts 17:26)."

Although there is only one race, however, God wanted ethnic and cultural differences within the human family. Paul's statement in Acts 17:26 continues, "that they should inhabit the whole earth; and *he determined the times set for them and the exact places where they should live.*"

Did you see that? God "determined the set times and exact places" where people would live. Differing regions of the world with different climates is the most likely explanation for the ethnic distinctions that eventually came into the human family. And the Bible says *God determined that!*

Being the student of Scripture that he was, Paul may have derived this idea from a statement tucked away in the song Moses taught the people of Israel just before his death: "When the Most High assigned lands to the nations, when He divided up the human race, he established the boundaries of the peoples..." (Deut. 32:8 NLT).

The origin of nations and cultures can be traced to a command God gave Noah, when he and his family came off the Ark: "Be fruitful and increase in number and *fill the earth*" (Gen. 9:1). According to Christopher Wright, the development of the nations recorded in Genesis 10 was the natural result of the "scattering" that occurred in obedience to that command.[4] But something happened that interrupted that process. Babel happened! In resistance to God's command to spread out, the people gathered "into a centralized

---

the introduction to this chapter. For more information on this topic, consult Joseph L. Graves, *The Race Myth: Why We Pretend Race Exists in America* and Michael Banton, *Racial Theories*, 2nd ed.

[4] Christopher J. H. Wright, *The Mission of God: Unlocking the Bible's Grand Narrative* (Downers Grove, IL: IVP Academic, 2008), 196.

location, thereby resisting God's purpose that they should multiply, fill the earth, and subdue it."[5]

Woodley believes the confusion of languages at Babel should not be viewed as a curse, but as the enforcement of God's original plan:

> God has planned since the beginning of time to cultivate diversity among human beings. When people tried to circumvent His plan, God intervened by creating many languages. Distinctions would have developed naturally over time, and changes would undoubtedly have taken place anyway if the people had spread out and obeyed God. His intervention merely sped up the process of developing the various ethnic groups that brought about His intended diversity.[6]

Theologian Walter Brueggemann concurs with Woodley, that the scattering of the people at Babel "is not negative nor concerned with punishment," but that "the intent of creation finally comes to fulfillment. Different families, tongues, lands, and nations are … part of [God's] will."[7] Brueggemann insists, however, that "there is a network of interrelatedness among all peoples. They belong to each other."[8]

While we're on the subject of Babel, let me share a remarkable observation from Rabbi Daniel Lapin. He says that Babel was an attempt at uniformity, citing their use of bricks, rather than stones, as a symbolic hint. Bricks speak of uniformity, each brick a man-made duplicate of every other brick. By contrast, every time God instructed people to build altars to Him, He called for uncut, natural stones, suggesting His preference for individuality and variety (Ex. 20:25). Babel, with its undisguised insistence on uniformity, stands as an example of the human tendency to fit everyone into the same mold, as

---

[5] Wright, 196.

[6] Woodley, *Living in Color*, 21.

[7] Walter Brueggemann, *Genesis*, Interpretation, a Bible Commentary for Teaching and Preaching (Atlanta: John Knox Press, 1982), 98–99.

[8] Brueggemann, 93.

a means of control. Thus, uniformity is a mechanism of tyranny. One lesson of the Babel story is clear: Humans like uniformity; God wants diversity.[9]

Diversity in the Church

Considering God's preference for diversity in everything else He made, it comes as no surprise that He desires the same for His Church. In light of Rabbi Lapin's stone-versus-brick metaphor above, consider the Apostle Peter's reference to members of the church as living stones: "You also, like living stones, are being built into a spiritual house to be a holy priesthood" (1 Pet. 2:5).

Using similar language, Paul calls the New Community "a holy temple in the Lord … *built together* into a dwelling place for God by the Spirit" (Eph. 2:21, 22). The word "stones" suggests individuality and diversity, while the phrase "built together" suggests unity. These twin themes, unity and diversity, are common in Paul's epistles. Commenting on this text, Gombis says, "Christ has created the new humanity made up of believers from any and every race and nation … Because of his victory in achieving peace (2:17), Christ has the right to build his temple, which stands as a lasting monument to his triumph (2:20-22)."[10]

In Ephesians 4, Paul changes the metaphor to that of a body, another apt illustration of unity and diversity (Eph. 4:4, 12, 16), one he develops more fully elsewhere: "The body is a unit, though it is made up of many parts; and though all its parts are many, they form one body. So it is with Christ. For we were all baptized by one Spirit into one body—whether Jews or Greeks, slave or free—and we were all given the one Spirit to drink. Now the body is not made up of one part but of many"

---

[9] Daniel Lapin, "The Role of the Church in Reshaping America" (presented at the Pastors' Briefing, Family Research Council, Washington, DC, May 2005).

[10] Gombis, "Ephesians 3:2-13," 322.

(1 Cor. 12:12-14). Paul's meaning is unmistakable. The Church enjoys the blessing of unity without the burden of uniformity.

As we have seen, God uses the Church to display His manifold (multi-colored) wisdom as well as His transforming, inclusive love for all people. Believers' fervent love for each other—and all others—stands in stark contrast to the selfish, shattered relationships of this world and attracts the hated and the hateful to the joyous fellowship of the Church.

Human Resistance to Diversity

This triumphant unity-within-diversity, to be showcased by the Church, would not come quickly or easily. The human context into which the Church was born was deeply divided. The ethnic and cultural differences between Jew and Gentile precluded social interaction, as we saw in Chapter Two. Jesus' first followers grew up in that culture of division, and it stained them deeply.

Jesus Resists the Resistance

For that reason, Jesus took measures to break the stranglehold of prejudice and prepare His followers to cross the cultural divide. Although His primary mission was to the "lost sheep of Israel," He demonstrated His all-inclusive love by healing a Samaritan leper (Luke 17:12-19), the daughter of a Canaanite woman (Matt. 15:22-28), and the servant of a Roman centurion (8:8-12). In fact, Jesus used the astonishing faith of that centurion as a teachable moment to help His disciples understand the eventual inclusion of Gentiles in the Kingdom. And, Jesus used a Samaritan as the ultimate example of neighbor-love (Luke 10:27-37). In one telling statement, he said, "I have other sheep, too, that are not in this sheepfold. I must bring them also. They will listen to my voice, and there will be one flock with one shepherd" (John 10:16 NLT).

Even in His selection of the Twelve, Jesus modeled inclusiveness. Although all of them were Jews, some of them were poles apart politically. William Steuart McBirnie makes the fascinating suggestion that James, the son of Alphaeus, was something of a Zealot, which would put him on the opposite end of the political spectrum from Matthew, his tax-collector brother. The influence of Jesus brought these estranged brothers together in a common faith and mission.[11]

Jesus' intentional emphasis on diversity and inclusiveness serves as bookends for His earthly ministry. In His inaugural message at Nazareth, He told the stories of Elijah and Elisha ministering to Gentiles, something that incited violent reaction. At his ascension, His parting words commissioned His disciples to take the good news across every conceivable cultural and national boundary to the "ends of the earth" (Acts 1:7-9).

The Lesson of Pentecost

Both Babel and Pentecost involved multiethnic, multinational, and multilingual elements. Despite their similarities, these seminal events differ vastly. Babel pictures confusion and separation. Pentecost suggests understanding and cohesion. At Babel, people moved away from each other into segregated living. At Pentecost, they came together into community. The distribution of languages at Pentecost and the response of the diverse audience who heard them, testify to the fact that God was pushing the Church to reach beyond one culture (Hebraic Jews) to many cultures.[12] Simply put, a lesson of Pentecost is that God wishes to include all kinds of people in the New Community. He wants a Church marked by unity *and* diversity, and He wants the Church to model that for the entire human family. In ages past *"he determined the times set for them and the exact places where they should live."*[13]

---

[11] William Steuart McBirnie, *The Search for the Twelve Apostles*, Living Books ed. (Carol Stream, IL: Tyndale House, 1987), 184.

[12] See Acts 2:5, 8-12.

[13] Acts 17:26

Since Pentecost, He wants us together in one delightfully diverse, yet beautifully unified body.

Acts: The Story of God's Relentless, Inclusive Love

Despite the inclusive ministry of Jesus and the instructive foreshadowing of Pentecost, "the eleven apostles carried racial residue from the deeply ingrained Jewish caste system. ... Although three years with Jesus had changed the eleven apostles significantly, they were still native-born Jews; ... racial residue still tainted them."[14] The book of Acts chronicles the Church's resistance to the inclusion of people other than Jews. It is also the story of God relentlessly pushing His people in that direction.

The Church began as a monocultural community, a few hundred Galileans and Judeans, whom I refer to as "Hebraic Jews" (to distinguish them from "Hellenistic Jews").[15] At Pentecost, thousands of Hellenistic Jews, visiting Jerusalem for the festival, came to faith in Christ through the preaching of Peter. Although they were accepted into the church, as far as we can tell, they were not given leadership roles. In other words, Pentecost failed to break the Hebraic monopoly on leadership in the Church. God would use sometimes harsh measures to force the church out of its monocultural mindset. Ethnic conflict in Acts 6 and persecution in Acts 7 and 8, difficult as they were, resulted in greater openness to diversity in the Church. In chapter 10, God resorted to a supernatural vision to free Peter from his prejudice and convince him to take the gospel to a Gentile household.

In their book *More Than Equals*, Spencer Perkins and Chris Rice point to six summary statements in Acts about the church's growth, each a

---

[14] Perkins and Rice, *More than Equals*, 153. Kindle ed., location 1654.

[15] The term "Hellenistic" refers to the Greek culture and language which was adopted by Jews of the Diaspora (dispersion). After the Exile, many Jews were dispersed throughout the Greek-speaking world, but would visit Jerusalem for annual festivals such as Passover and Pentecost. These Hellenistic Jews were sometimes viewed with suspicion by Galileans and Judeans, and vice versa.

"landmark event, a turning point for the church," each a milestone in the church's movement toward diversity.[16] Take a minute and study the table below. You might be amazed at the correlation between these events and their effect on the growth of the church!

Landmark Event	Significance	Summary Statement
Pentecost	Multinational ingathering (Most of the pilgrims at Pentecost were Jews, not Gentiles. However, after their baptism in the Spirit, many became missionaries to their respective nations.)	"And the Lord added to their number daily those who were being saved" (Acts 2:47)
First Deacons Appointed (all of them Greek in language and culture)	Greek-speaking leadership introduced to the Jerusalem Church	"So the word of God spread. The number of disciples in Jerusalem increased rapidly, and a large number of priests became obedient to the faith" (Acts 6:7)
Stephen (a Greek-speaking Deacon) Preaches His "Uncircumcised Hearts" Sermon and is Martyred	After Stephen's death, believers are scattered by persecution and take the Gospel to non-Jews	"Those who had been scattered preached the word wherever they went" (Acts 8:4)

---

[16] Perkins and Rice, *More than Equals*, Kindle ed., Locations 1705-1915.

Philip (a Greek-speaking Deacon) Evangelizes Samaria	Philip bridges the cultural divide with the Gospel	"Then the church… was strengthened; and encouraged by the Holy Spirit, it grew in numbers, living in the fear of the Lord" (Acts 9:31)
Peter Obeys Divine Revelation and Preaches to Cornelius' Household	Gentiles are filled with the Holy Spirit and received into the Church	"But the word of God continued to increase and spread" (Acts12:24)
The Jerusalem Council	Gentiles are given full status in the Church without circumcision	"So the churches were strengthened in the faith and grew daily in numbers" (Acts 16:5)

Can you imagine the culture shock these "landmark events" must have caused the Hebraic Jews through whom Jesus had founded the Church? Think about the radical shift they produced in their understanding of the Church. Yet, each time they abandoned their prejudice and opened their hearts to people different from themselves, God showed His profound pleasure by increasing the Church's numbers and influence. In other words, embracing diversity resulted in substantial advances for the Church, time and again.

Antioch: A New Pattern for the Church

A major pivot in the Acts story occurs in chapter 11. Members of the Jerusalem church fled 300 miles north to Syrian Antioch, due to the martyrdom of Stephen and the persecution that followed. Antioch was the third largest city in the Roman Empire (after Rome and

Alexandria).[17] "Antioch was a prosperous commercial center [and] ... a meeting point of the Greek and oriental civilizations."[18]

Can't you sense the influence of the Spirit in this, leading these disciples to such a strategic location? As soon as they arrived, they "began to speak to Greeks also, telling them the good news about the Lord Jesus. The Lord's hand was with them, and a great number of people believed and turned to the Lord" (Acts 11:20-21). The statement, "the Lord's hand was with them," evidences God's favor on this cross-cultural evangelism. Perkins and Rice describe the church that resulted from it:

> The Antioch church broke new ground: it was the first true multiracial church, headed by strong multiracial leadership. ... This multiracial fellowship became God's headquarters for expanding the frontiers of the gospel. From the beginning, unlike the Jerusalem church, Antioch was an intentional missionary church. No prodding was needed, no persecution necessary, no time wasted.[19]

In reading the book of Acts, it's easy to skim right through chapter 11 and miss the significance of what is happening. But, if you read it thoughtfully, you can't avoid seeing its significance. For one thing, the rest of Acts is all about the activities that originated in Antioch. In fact, it's no exaggeration to say that the Antioch church replaced the Jerusalem church as the focal point of God's work in the world. Here's why: First, the believers at Antioch, in response to the Spirit's leading, launched the missionary enterprise that ultimately evangelized Europe.[20] Second, at Antioch, Paul confronted Peter's lapse into Jewish monoculturalism, from which the Jerusalem Council was

---

[17] James F. Strange, "Antioch," in *Holman Bible Dictionary*, ed. Trent C. Butler (Nashville, TN: Holman Bible Publishers, 1991), 64.

[18] Glanville Downey, "Antioch (Syrian)," in *The International Standard Bible Encyclopedia*, ed. Geoffrey W. Bromiley, vol. 1, fully revised edition (Grand Rapids, MI: Eerdmans, 1979), 142.

[19] Perkins and Rice, *More than Equals*, 169. Kindle ed., location 1797.

[20] Acts 13:1-3

convened, giving Gentiles full status in the Church.[21] Third, what God did in and through the Antioch church assured that Christianity would become far more than a mere sect of Judaism.

So, the Antioch church proved catalytic, not only for the advancement of the gospel, but also for the changing character of the Church, something hinted at in a new name applied to believers there. "The disciples were called Christians first at Antioch" (Acts 11:26). In short, God used the Antioch church to ensure the multiethnic, multicultural, and multinational character of His Church.

One of Antioch's greatest contributions was the impact it made on Saul of Tarsus. Immediately after Saul's conversion, Jesus spoke of him in a prophetic vision to Ananias of Damascus: "This man is my chosen instrument to carry my name before the Gentiles" (Acts 9:15). Without a doubt, Paul's experience with multicultural believers at Antioch helped prepare him for that assignment. Although Peter was God's first instrument to the Gentiles, Paul would surpass him in championing that mission. To say the least, Antioch provided the church model that would inform Paul's teaching and writing for the rest of his life. In summation, the Antioch model suggests that a multi-ethnic body better reflects God's intention for the Church.

~~~~~~~~~~~~

In this chapter, we have seen how God designed diversity into the created order and into the human family. Evidently, He considers diversity beautiful and desirable. We have also seen how God pushes His people to embrace diversity in the Church. This is because He loves people in every nation and culture, people of every language and ethnicity and skin color. Pastor Craig Groeschel of LifeChurch.tv, observes, "As the diversity of our culture continues to increase,

---

[21] Galatians 2:11-21; Acts 15

Christ's Church has not been keeping pace in many parts of the world. If I can be so bold to speak on behalf of God, I truly believe He wants this to change. The most diverse place in the world will be heaven. It's time for a little heaven on earth."[22]

Pastors hold the key to intentional diversity in their congregations. Scott Williams says, "As a pastor, I can't force people of different ethnicities to come through the doors of my church; however, I can force the bold conversations with staff, volunteers, and congregants."[23] Williams recommends that pastors preach on the divine delight in diversity and the pastoral staff model it through interracial friendships.[24]

Admittedly, some churches do not have the option of diversity, such as those in rural, monocultural communities. However, demographic trends suggest that those communities might become increasingly rare.[25] Meanwhile, many churches in America have the option—and now, the mandate—to intentionally reach out to people of every race and culture who surround their campuses. Doing so will serve as a giant step toward reconciliation in their communities and will create the potential for interracial *koinonia.*

That being said, diversity in a church presents challenges. Our differences can be a breeding ground for misunderstanding and mistrust, for fear and prejudice. Our differences can cause us to distance ourselves from each other. The best way to overcome that is to understand our differences, to look them square in the face. So, let's move on to Part 2 and take an honest look at ourselves.

---

[22] Scott Williams, *Church Diversity: Sunday the Most Segregated Day of the Week* (Green Forest, AR: New Leaf Press, 2011), Kindle e–book, location 176.

[23] Williams, location 1101.

[24] Williams, location 2232.

[25] Robert Bernstein, *U.S. Census Bureau Projections Show a Slower Growing, Older, More Diverse Nation a Half Century from Now*, Press Release (United States Census Bureau, December 12, 2012), http://www.census.gov/newsroom/releases/archives/population/cb12-243.html.

Part 2
Exploring the Divide

When engineers are planning to build a bridge across a chasm, they first go down into the chasm to explore it. They need to know its width and depth. They need to know the terrain and topography, and even more importantly, what lies beneath the surface of the terrain.

Similarly, if we are to build bridges of reconciliation and fellowship across the racial divide, we would be wise to do some exploring. As we do, we will discover that the gap is wider and deeper than race, ethnicity, or skin color. It involves culture, history, and the "grand canyon of division"—politics. It involves ongoing racial insensitivity, corporate pain, and racialization.

Such exploration will not be easy or comfortable. At times, it will be downright painful and even a little dangerous. It might call into question some things we have been so sure of, and force us out of our comfort zones. Our venture into history may be traumatic for some, because for them, it will be anything but a "stroll down memory lane."

But, traveling through that rough terrain is worth it, because the journey leads to *koinonia*!

Come on, let's explore together!

4

CULTURE:
Seeing Life through Different Lenses

"If we could stop assuming that other people are like us—if we could begin to believe that we don't necessarily understand how others are thinking and that they don't always understand how we are thinking—then we would be well on our way to avoiding cultural misunderstandings and all the problems they give rise to." Craig Storti

It was six men of Indostan to learning much inclined,
Who went to see the Elephant (though all of them were blind),
That each by observation might satisfy his mind.

The **First** approached the Elephant, and happening to fall
Against his broad and sturdy side, at once began to bawl:
"God bless me! But the Elephant is very like a WALL!"

The **Second,** feeling of the tusk, cried, "Ho, what have we here,
So very round and smooth and sharp? to me 'tis might clear
This wonder of an Elephant is very like a SPEAR!"

The **Third** approached the animal, and happening to take
The squirming trunk within his hands, thus boldly up and spake:
"I see," quoth he, "the Elephant is very like a SNAKE!"

The **Fourth** reached out an eager hand, and felt about the knee
"What most this wondrous beast is like is mighty plain," quoth he:
"'Tis clear enough the Elephant is very like a TREE!"

The **Fifth,** who chanced to touch the ear, said: "E'en the blindest man
Can tell what this resembles most; deny the fact who can?
This marvel of an Elephant is very like a FAN!"

The **Sixth** no sooner had begun about the beast to grope,
Than seizing on the swinging tail that fell within his scope,
"I see" quoth he, "the Elephant is very like a ROPE!"

And so these men of Indostan disputed loud and long,
Each in his own opinion exceeding stiff and strong,
Though each was partly in the right, and all were in the wrong!

—John Godfrey Saxe[1]

The racial divide in America involves more than race and ethnicity. Cultural differences also figure into the misunderstandings that fuel division. Often, we define the term "cross-cultural" as "international." Today, the term is being applied more and more to relationships between Americans. And increasingly, culture is having an impact on relationships within the Body of Christ. Learning to respect and appreciate each other's cultures is not only possible, it is essential to our unity!

There are probably as many definitions of the word "culture" as there are recipes for stew. Patty Lane defines culture as, "a system of meanings and values that shape one's behavior."[2] According to Edgar Schein, "Culture is to a group what personality is to an individual. Elements of culture are passed to new members and future generations of the group."[3] One of the simplest definitions for culture I have encountered is "the way we do things around here."

Cultural peculiarities show up readily when people of different races or nationalities worship and fellowship together. These differences can

---

[1] John Godfrey Saxe, "The Blind Men and the Elephant," in *The Best Loved Poems of the American People*, ed. Hazel Fellman (Garden City, NY: Garden City Books, 1936), 521–22.

[2] Patty Lane, *A Beginner's Guide to Crossing Cultures: Making Friends in a Multicultural World* (Downers Grove, IL: InterVarsity Press, 2002), Kindle e–book, locations 205-209.)

[3] Edgar H. Schein, *Organizational Culture and Leadership*, 4th ed. (San Francisco, CA: Jossey-Bass, 2010), 36.

involve music preference, tastes in clothing, degree of formality or casualness in gatherings, and concepts of time, particularly what it means to be "on time." Failure to understand each other's culture can lead to misjudgments of character. Lane observes, "The more obvious the difference between people, the quicker the tendency to form stereotypes."[4]

The need for cross-cultural understanding in American life has never been greater, and it is not limited to black-white racial differences. The demographics of America are changing at an almost unbelievable pace, and these shifting demographics have brought the mission field to the front door of the Church! Yet that mission field presents definite challenges, and cultural differences is one of the biggest.

The "Browning of America"

Sociologists have coined the phrase "the browning of America" to describe current and coming demographic trends in the population. "White babies are no longer a majority of new births, according to the Census Bureau. America is quietly 'browning.'"[5]

A *New York Times* blog states:

> The census calculates that by 2042, Americans who identify themselves as Hispanic, Black, Asian, American Indian, Native Hawaiian and Pacific Islander will together outnumber ... whites. Four years ago, officials had projected the shift would come in 2050. The main reason for the accelerating change is significantly higher birthrates among immigrants. Another factor is the influx of foreigners, rising ... to more than 2 million a year by midcentury. ... "No other country has experienced such rapid

---

[4] Lane, Location 322.
[5] Clarence Page, "Adjusting to the 'Browning' of America," *San Diego Union Tribune*, May 26, 2012, http://www.utsandiego.com/news/2012/may/26/tp-adjusting-to-the-browning-of-america/?page=2#article.

racial and ethnic change," said Mark Mather, a demographer with the Population Reference Bureau, a research organization in Washington.[6]

Immigration Stats: Did You Know?

Take a moment to ponder the following:

- 75% of those entering the labor force in the U.S. are ethnic minorities.
- As baby boomers are retiring, the majority of Social Security contributions come from minorities.
- 45% of students in public schools are minorities.
- Los Angeles is now the second largest Iranian city in the world.
- Chicago has more Poles than San Francisco has people.
- One-third of the world's Jews live in the USA.
- There are more Buddhists than Episcopalians in the USA.
- 239 languages are spoken in California / 184 in NY / 181 in Washington / 169 in Texas.
- NYC has more than 350,000 Dominicans. The capital city of DR has only 225,000.
- 8 million Muslims in the US, increasing at a rate of 200,000 per year. 2000 mosques and Islamic centers across the USA.[7]
- More than 400,000 international students from 181 countries study at American universities.[8]
- "Since the 1700s, the most common last name in America was Smith. Now, it's Rodriguez.[9]

---

[6] Sam Roberts, "Minorities in U.S. Set to Become Majority by 2042," *New York Times Blog America*, accessed August 4, 2012, http://www.nytimes.com/2008/08/14/world/americas/14iht-census.1.15284537.html.

[7] Johan Mostert, "Global & Community Leadership" (class notes for Core 3 course at Assemblies of God Theological Seminary, Springfield, MO, June 7, 2011), 8-9.

[8] Lane, Locations 161-173.

[9] James Emery White, *Meet Generation Z: Understanding and Reaching the New Post-Christian World* (Grand Rapids, MI: Baker Books, 2017) 45.

For many years, America has been described as a "melting pot." Patty Lane prefers another metaphor to better explain the rich, demographic mixture in modern American life:

> Think about stew. In a stew pot the potatoes look like potatoes and taste like potatoes, but with the added savor of carrots, onions and beef. Each ingredient takes on some of the flavor of the other ingredients, without becoming invisible. Thus, the entire dish is more delicious and each ingredient is enhanced. The United States is like stew. The individual cultures are recognizable, yet they influence each other and the flavors mix together. It is easy to see in this image the advantage of stew over soup that has been pureed into a uniform consistency. As connoisseurs of food we know which has the most appeal. Yet when it comes to culture many times we seem to want the pureed version, even though we will lose the rich textures, colors and unique flavors.[10]

Lane's statement doesn't deny the need for an overarching American culture defined by a common language (English) and common values such as those spelled out in the Constitution of the United States. As long as Americans—regardless of their ethnicity or national origin—identify *as Americans* and determine to stick together, our cultural variety and richness will enhance the exceptionalism of America.[11]

Understanding a Few Key Terms

I don't mean to get academic on you, but a look at a few sociological terms can open our eyes to some of the challenges of understanding other cultures. Hang with me as we explore the meanings of these terms and look at some examples. I think you'll find this interesting.

> **Xenophobia** (pronounced "zeno-fobia") = "Fear of another culture." People tend to fear what they don't understand, and fear leads to prejudice. The word xenophobia is a sociological

---

[10] Lane, Locations 187-194.

[11] "Pluralism," the notion that all cultures are equal in terms of their values and worldview, is false. Cultures strongly influenced by biblical faith espouse more excellent societal values than cultures where the Bible has never gained a foothold. Pluralism in its absolute sense leads to the disintegration of society.

term that comes from two Greek words, *xenos* (stranger) and *phobos* (fear). Literally, it means, "fear of strangers." Contrast this word with "hospitality," a word used by Paul in Romans 12:3: "Share with God's people who are in need. Practice *hospitality*." The word "hospitality" is the English translation of the Greek word *philoxenia*, which literally means, "love of strangers" (*phileo* = love and *xenos* = stranger). Instead of fearing people different from ourselves, the Bible exhorts us to love them!

Stereotype = "A skewed perspective that tends to restrict and accuse."[12] Stereotypes occur when someone makes an observation about a few members of a culture, and then applies that observation to everyone in that culture. Patty Lane says, "Often the observation is true of the few people observed..., but to generalize that quality to all the members of the group creates a box, which limits the way in which others of that group will be seen. It allows people outside the group to decide who the others are without having to consider who that individual person is. ... Ethnic jokes, derogatory comments and idioms that are based on a stereotype create barriers to real relationships."[13] Here are examples of stereotype: "Black people have natural rhythm." "Jews are rich." "Men are better drivers." "Muslims are terrorists." For other examples of stereotypes, see "Black-to-White Stereotypes" and "White-to-Black Stereotypes" in my book *Journey to Koinonia: An Interracial Small Group Experience*.

Misattribution = "The tendency to judge other people's behavior by one's own cultural experience."[14] For example, in modern western culture, refusal to look someone in the eye while speaking to them is often perceived as being either devious or disrespectful. Conversely, in certain non-western cultures, looking someone directly in the eye is considered disrespectful, especially if the person is speaking to someone of a higher social order. Patty Lane offers the following example of misattribution:

---

[12] Lane, Locations 161-173.
[13] Lane, Locations 328-333.
[14] Lane, Location 348.

Two pastors met at a conference and introduced themselves. The first one said, "Hello, I am Ralph Jones, pastor of the Downtown Christian Church." His new acquaintance said, "It is nice to meet you. I am Pastor Jong Kim, of First Korean Church in Scottsdale." While having lunch together, they ran into a colleague of Pastor Jones. Ralph introduced his new Korean friend, "Jong, I would like you to meet John, an old friend of mine from college." Placing his hand on Jong's shoulder, he continued, "Jong is a fellow pastor whom I have just met." Although Pastor Kim said nothing, he felt disrespected by the way Ralph introduced him. In the Korean culture, pastors are shown a great deal of respect and are always introduced and referred to by a title, such as doctor, pastor, or reverend. To be treated in a familiar way by a person he barely knew communicated disrespect.

This is a clear case of misattribution. Pastor Kim misattributed Ralph's behavior because he didn't know that in Ralph's culture, such "familiarity" simply conveys friendliness and warmth.[15] Lane observes, "Repeat this scenario over and over, thousands of times a day, and you have a glimpse of what we are facing in building relationships with persons of other cultures within the United States. Racism is real and it is destructive and wrong, but one place to begin to eliminate it is to begin to understand cultural differences."[16]

Ethno-centrism = "The belief that one's own culture is superior to all others." People naturally assume that the way their group does something is the "right" way, and therefore, any other way of doing it is inferior. Ethno-centrism often manifests as sarcastic derision of the way people of other cultures dress, speak, behave, eat, or think. When we see their ways as not just different, but "weird," or "dumb," we are guilty of what Jim Lo calls "cultural arrogance."[17]

---

[15] Lane, Locations 378-383.

[16] Lane, Locations 205-209.

[17] Jim Lo, *Intentional Diversity: Creating Cross-Cultural Ministry Relationships in Your Church* (Indianapolis, IN: Wesleyan Publishing House, 2002), 43.

Points to Ponder:

To which do you tend to lean, xenophobia (fear of other cultures) or *philoxenia* (showing hospitality to strangers)? Do you sometimes find yourself using stereotypes to describe people of other ethnicities or countries? What examples of misattribution have you seen in cross-cultural relationships? Have there been instances where you have misattributed someone else's words or behavior?

Reflect on the following statement by David Ireland: "Most Christians' worship habits are culturally learned and not necessarily strictly biblical. There is no precisely right or wrong way to worship God. The problem is that people think of their own style as 'the Bible way.'"[18] Do you agree with Ireland? Why or why not?

The Six Lenses of Culture

John Godfrey Saxe's poem, "The Blind Men and the Elephant" (at the beginning of this chapter), delightfully illustrates the fact that different people "see" the same thing in different ways. It also suggests that we are all blind in some ways. Like when it comes to seeing our own culture. As I pointed out in chapter one, any culture serves as an invisible veil to those in the culture, because to them, it's not "culture," it's "just the way things are." However, when we intentionally choose to take a look at life through other cultural lenses, we not only see those cultures, we begin to see and better understand our own.

As we learned in the definitions above, our cultural differences can create gaps in understanding, and those gaps can fuel unhealthy, divisive attitudes chock full of stereotypes and misattributions. These faulty ways of viewing people can be corrected by what Patty Lane calls the "six lenses of culture." She observes,

---

[18] Ireland, *What Color Is Your God? A New Approach to Developing a Multicultural Lifestyle*, 158–59.

Each culture has a unique way of seeing life and relationships. When we understand our own cultural lenses and the lenses of others, we are more likely to make friends with persons of other cultures. These lenses will provide a framework through which we can understand and build healthy cross-cultural relationships. There are six dimensions of culture that provide cultural lenses necessary for understanding the specific aspects of any culture.[19]

Each cultural lens can open a window of understanding into another's world:

(1) Context. The context lens refers to where and how something is done—the visible trappings of an event or activity. *High-context* cultures place as much value on the setting in which an event occurs as the event itself. For example, Sunday worship services, ceremonies, rites of passage, and other memorable occasions must be celebrated in grand style. Thus, dressy attire, protocol, and reverential treatment of authority figures are essential to the occasion. On the other hand, *low-context* cultures tend to diminish the trappings of such events and focus more on the content of the occasion.

(2) Activity. The Activity Lens has to do with whether a culture emphasizes being or doing. *Doing* cultures value results and productivity. *Being* cultures value relationships and quality of life.

(3) Authority. The Authority Lens governs the way a culture defines and understands authority. In *hierarchical* cultures, rank or family connections determines one's position. In *egalitarian* cultures, all persons have equal value and recognition results from individual achievement.

(4) Source of Identity. The Source of Identity Lens denotes whether a culture is collective or individualistic in nature. "*Collective* cultures view themselves as part of a group, which usually is their family, tribe, or community. As a result, people in these cultures relate to persons

---

[19] Lane, Locations 649–1642. Lane's book is the source of all six "cultural lenses" discussed in this section.

not only as unique individuals but as part of a greater whole." In collective cultures, one's sense of identity is tied to their group.

Most people who as a group have experienced oppression, have a collective mindset. For example, after the Israeli Six-Day War, Rabbi Lord Jonathan Sacks, the former Chief Rabbi of England, wrote:

> "I had witnessed something in those days and weeks that didn't make sense in the rest of my world. ... It had to do with Jewish identity. Collectively, the Jewish people had looked in the mirror and said, we are still Jews. ... It meant that they felt part of a people, involved in its fate, implicated in its destiny, caught up in its tragedy, exhilarated by its survival. ... It was then I knew that being Jewish was not something private and personal but something collective and historical ... part of an extended family ... connected by bonds of kinship and responsibility."[20]

Another example of collective thinking is the way people in the black community sometimes react when an injustice happens to a black person. Even if they don't know the individual, they feel connected to them, and they experience something Alice Patterson calls "corporate pain," a concept we will consider in more depth in chapter six.

Conversely, *individualistic* cultures see each person as a stand-alone individual whose identity is not dependent on family or community. Argentine Evangelist Ed Silvoso observes that "white folks are one of the few people-groups who do not have a people-group mentality."[21]

(5) Temporal. The Temporal Lens affects the way a culture views time. Many Westerners view time as limited, segmented, and precisely measured, while most of the world sees time as fluid, flexible, and historical. Arriving "late" for a function may not necessarily be due to tardiness or carelessness. In some cases, it could simply be a different view of the meaning of time. Taking into account the temporal lens can help those who insist on being "on time" have a little more

---

[20] Rabbi Lord Jonathan Sacks, *Radical Then, Radical Now*, quoted in *The Six-Day War: The Story of Yom Yerushalayim and the Six Days of Deliverance* by Hagi Ben-Artzi.

[21] Ed Silvoso, *Prayer Evangelism: How to Change the Spiritual Climate over Your Home, Neighborhood, and City* (Ventura, CA: Regal Books, 2000), Kindle e-book, 137.

patience with those who view the starting time in relative terms. This is especially important in multi-racial or international churches.

Also, according to Patty Lane, "In the historical view of time, one's history is always present in the now." This explains why many black people have an intense interest in their African heritage—their "roots." It also explains why they cannot forget the injustices their forebears suffered under slavery and Jim Crow. Some white people perceive this as a "chip-on-the-shoulder" mentality, and want their black friends to "just get over it." However, if white people understood the temporal lens, they would know that their black friends see themselves as part of their history. It is a huge component of their present identity. Telling them to "get over it" makes as little sense as telling a Jewish person to get over the Holocaust. (Bear this in mind as you read about "Our Shared History" in the next chapter.)

(6) Worldview. A culture's worldview determines its perception of reality. Generally speaking, three broad perspectives of reality exist in the world today: Pre-modern, Modern, and Post-modern. To these we might add Rationalist, Secularist, Religious, and Superstitious. Of course, believers who see the Bible as divinely inspired and authoritative, hold to a *Biblical* worldview.[22]

Understanding each other's "cultural lenses" will cause "all kinds of things to make sense that initially were mysterious, frustrating, or seemingly stupid."[23] When we appreciate why those in another culture do what they do, instead of deriding their behavior as "weird," we grow as human beings. In the words of Edgar Schein, "Understanding cultural forces enables us to understand ourselves better."[24]

---

[22] Lane, Locations 649–1642. Lane's book is the source of all six "cultural lenses" discussed in this section.
[23] Schein, 32.
[24] Schein, 26.

Similarly, when black and white Christians seek to understand each other in light of their cultural contexts, they will judge each other less and appreciate each other more.

Points to Ponder:

In some African American churches, there is a preference for elaborate ceremonies, dressy attire, and reverential titles. By contrast, more and more white churches are moving away from such formalities. Ponder this in light of the lenses of culture. Which of the six lenses addresses this?

Would you agree with me that God expects more of Christians than merely tolerating each other's cultures? Think about that in light of the following statements:

- "God created culture and the vast assortment of cultures present today are a reflection of his love of diversity. ... There is a profound witness given when people from great diversity come together through the power and love of God."[25]

- "God can be properly revealed only through diversity."[26]

- As in the case of the blind men and the elephant, in the Church it takes all of us, with our different ways and perspectives, to fully appreciate the vastness of our awesome God!

Do you agree? Why or why not?

Either way, I hope you will keep reading. We're about to journey through sacred ground. Let's tread lightly, because what follows may recall sad stories some have heard from their parents and grandparents. Some of it may even conjure painful memories of their own.

---

[25] Lane, location 2484.

[26] Duane Elmer, *Cross-Cultural Conflict: Building Relationships for Effective Ministry* (Downers Grove, IL: InterVarsity Press, 1993), 13.

5

OUR SHARED HISTORY:
Walking Softly over Sacred Ground

"Because of our history of segregation, Jim Crowism, and racism,
generations of African-Americans have grown up with a sense of alienation
toward their own country."
Dr. Ben Carson
" We didn't land on Plymouth Rock. Plymouth Rock landed on us."[1]
Malcolm X

Black and white Christians not only approach each other from different cultural perspectives, they also view history—particularly American history—in decidedly different lights. For this reason, a truthful examination of the nation's history—the good and the bad—will heighten our understanding of each other. In some sense, we are all the products of our history. "We learn our history not to change or avenge the past, but to understand our present so we can have a say in our future."[2]

In general, white Christians cherish patriotic feelings about America's early history, proudly citing its biblical moorings and the daring genius of its founders. Many black Christians, on the other hand, view that same history through the prism of oppression and injustice, and as a result, carry heavy emotional baggage. Dr. Ben Carson says, "Because of our history of segregation, Jim Crowism, and racism, generations of

---

[1] *The Second Chance*, directed by Steve Taylor, DVD (Sony Pictures, 2006).

[2] Glenn Usry and Craig S Keener, *Black Man's Religion: Can Christianity Be Afrocentric?* (Downers Grove, IL: InterVarsity Press, 1996), Kindle e–book, location 131.

African-Americans have grown up with a sense of alienation toward their own country. This has created extreme levels of cynicism and distrust among many citizens who might otherwise have been enthusiastic supporters of the nation."[3]

America's Godly and Ungodly Heritage

In 1831, Frenchman Alexis de Tocqueville came to America to study the secrets of her success. He noted that America's public schools, unlike those in Europe, used the Holy Bible extensively.[4] He also offered the following reflection: "Not until I went into the churches of America and heard her pulpits flame with righteousness did I understand the secret of her genius and power. America is great because America is good, and if America ever ceases to be good, America will cease to be great."[5]

De Tocqueville's glowing tribute omits the dark side of early American history, particularly as it relates to the treatment of black people. Early America was not good to its black residents.

> Immigrants from many countries have come to the United States in search of the 'American Dream.' African Americans differed from all other ethnic groups in that they did not willingly come to North America, nor was the 'American Dream' made available to them. The predominant distinguishing factor for African Americans is the history of social, economic, and political oppression experienced because of color discrimination.[6]

Paradoxically, black people have been good to America. Many white people remain unaware of the contributions African Americans made to the founding and development of this nation. For example, the first

---

[3] Ben Carson, *America the Beautiful: Rediscovering What Made This Nation Great* (Grand Rapids, MI: Zondervan, 2012), 116.

[4] Carson, *America the Beautiful*, 57.

[5] William J. Federer, *America's God and Country: Encyclopedia of Quotations* (St. Louis, MO: Amerisearch, 2000), 206.

[6] James Breckenridge and Lillian Breckenridge, *What Color Is Your God? Multicultural Education in the Church* (Grand Rapids, MI: Baker Books, 1998), 217.

man to die in the American struggle for independence was a black seaman named Crispus Attucks.[7] Black and white minutemen fought side-by-side at Bunker Hill, and black soldiers from all thirteen colonies fought in the Revolutionary War.[8]

The discoveries of black scientist George Washington Carver once revived the economy of the South.[9] Black physicians performed the first successful heart surgeries and developed the method of separating and storing blood plasma, saving thousands of Americans in World War II.[10] Black inventors improved the American standard of living with products such as traffic signals, affordable shoes, refrigeration systems, and microphone chips.[11] Despite these and many other contributions by blacks, America did not reciprocate in kind.

Jamestown or Plymouth—Which Vision for America?

Before discussing the tragedy of African slavery, let me state that I do not subscribe to the notion that America was founded on slavery and is therefore fundamentally flawed. The "1619 Project," a cadre of writers and journalists, make just such a claim, asserting that 1619 was the year African slaves arrived in Jamestown, the first permanent English colony in America. The 1619 Project sees the American narrative as a story of systemic racial injustice, from its earliest founding.

In actual fact, the Africans who arrived in Jamestown in 1619 were no longer slaves. They had been rescued from a Portuguese slave ship in the West Indies by the crew of a British privateer, the White Lion. They were then brought to Jamestown, and were allowed to work as

---

[7] Martin Luther King, Jr., *The Trumpet of Conscience* (Boston, MA: Beacon Press, 2010), Kindle e–book, location 18.)

[8] Spencer Perkins and Chris Rice, *More Than Equals: Racial Healing for the Sake of the Gospel* (Downers Grove, IL: InterVarsity Press, 2000), Kindle e–book, location 1152.

[9] Martin Luther King, Jr., *Where Do We Go from Here: Chaos or Community?* (Boston, MA: Beacon Press, 1968), Kindle e–book, location 580.

[10] King, Jr., *Where Do We Go from Here?*, location 580.

[11] Carson, *America the Beautiful*, 116.

indentured servants alongside white indentured servants.[12] That same year, the Jamestown colony established their General Assembly, which became a model for representative governments in later colonies.

Nevertheless, Jamestown is hardly an example of American virtue. It had been established by the Virginia Company for one purpose—to search for gold and silver deposits in the New World and a trade route to the Orient. Jamestown was first and foremost, a commercial venture.

Contrast that with another seminal event that happened in 1620. A congregation of Christian believers seeking religious freedom landed at Plymouth, Massachusetts. Persecuted for their faith by the Church of England, these pilgrims braved treacherous seas and suffered intense privation to live in a country where they could worship God according to the dictates of their consciences. The founding purpose of their colony is preserved in their first governing document, the Mayflower Compact: "Having undertaken for the Glory of God, and Advancement of the Christian Faith … a Voyage to plant the first Colony in the northern Parts of Virginia…"

Those first two American colonies—Jamestown and Plymouth—were founded for very different reasons, and they represent two very different visions for America. One was about gold and the other about God. Slavery would come to America in the 1680s, because some Americans sought after gold. Slavery would eventually be abolished, because other Americans sought after God.

There are those who seek to frame the American story as the relentless pursuit of material gain for the few, at the cost of untold suffering by the many. That there have been long episodes of such is undeniable, as I will show. But, to see America only in that light is to ignore the lives and labor of countless godly people—black and white—who prayed and preached and bled and died to establish a land of freedom and faith for all people. It ignores the great spiritual revivals that, time

---

[12] Indentured servitude was a form of labor in which a person agreed to work for his creditor for a specified number of years to repay his loan. In colonial times, it was a way for a person to pay for his transportation to America.

and again, awakened the nation's conscience, not only to sin and salvation, but also to matters of justice and righteousness. It also ignores the ongoing efforts of Americans who have worked to right America's wrongs, to end oppression, and to insure "liberty and justice for all."

So, as you read the following horrific accounts of American slavery and Jim Crow laws, please understand that my purpose is not to paint America as fundamentally flawed. With all our sins—past and present—there is much about America that is noble and good. Millions of immigrants still come to these shores seeking a better life, a testament to the fact that, when it comes to nations, America is still the world's best hope. Having said that, there is value in candidly facing the brutal truth about our past, not to wallow in guilt, but to guarantee a better future.

Slavery

Martin Luther King, Jr. observed that American slavery was different from other forms of slavery "because it consciously dehumanized the Negro."[13] Unlike the Greco-Roman version which preserved family life, American slavery destroyed families, beginning on the coasts of Africa:

> Because the middle passage was long and expensive, African families were torn apart in the interest of selectivity, as if the members were beasts. In the ships' holds, Black captives were packed spoon fashion to live on a voyage often lasting two to six months in a space for each the size of a coffin. If water ran short, or famine threatened, or a plague broke out, whole cargoes of living and dead were thrown overboard. The sheer physical torture was sufficient to murder millions of men, women and children. But even more incalculable was the psychological damage. Of those families who survived the voyage, many more were ripped apart on the auction block as soon as they reached American shores. Against this ghastly background the Negro family began life in the United States. On the plantation ... [they experienced] the repetitive tearing apart of families as children, husbands or wives were sold to other plantations.[14]

---

[13] King, Jr., *Where Do We Go from Here?*, location 1260.
[14] King, Jr., *Where Do We Go from Here?*, locations 1260–66.

Frederick Douglass' heart-rending account of his relationship with his mother illustrates the emotional pain millions of slaves experienced:

> I never saw my mother, to know her as such, more than four or five times in my life; and each of these times was very short in duration, and at night. She was hired by Mr. Stewart, who lived about twelve miles from my home. She made her journeys to see me in the night, travelling the whole distance on foot, after the performance of her day's work. She was a field hand, and a whipping is the penalty of not being in the field at sunrise. ... She would lie down with me, and get me to sleep, but long before I waked she was gone.[15]

Douglass' mother finally succumbed to these stresses when he was only seven, yet he was not allowed to visit her during her illness or even attend her burial. Similar stories could be told of other slaves, illustrating the fact that American slavery involved more than back-breaking labor in the sun. It deprived its victims of the most basic human freedoms. Fear of a possible slave revolt led to laws prohibiting slaves from learning to read and write[16] or even to assemble for their own worship services.[17] Any resistance or complaint about such conditions could result in severe beatings, mutilation, or death.[18] History documents that slaves were whipped and punished just for gathering to pray.[19] "The slaves, ... had to steal away to clandestine prayer meetings in their cabins, woods, thickets, hollows, and brush arbors, the aptly named 'hush harbors.'"[20]

---

[15] Frederick Douglass, "From Narrative of the Life of Frederick Douglass, An American Slave," in *Growing Up Black: From Slave Days to the Present*, ed. Jay David, rev. (New York, NY: Avon Books, 1992), 83–84.

[16] Martin Luther King, Jr., *Why We Can't Wait* (Boston, MA: Beacon Press, 1964), Kindle e–book, location 346.

[17] Usry and Keener, *Black Man's Religion*, location 1295.

[18] King, Jr., *Why We Can't Wait*, location 346.

[19] Cheryl Jeanne Sanders, *Saints in Exile: The Holiness-Pentecostal Experience in African American Religion and Culture* (New York: Oxford University Press, 1996), Kindle e–book, location 253.

[20] Sanders, *Saints in Exile*, location 253.

The irony of Christian slave masters beating Christian slaves for exercising their faith defies understanding, and leaves one wondering how slaves could hold onto their faith. Milton Sernett comments, "To hold to Christianity while receiving blows from its professed practitioners, to avoid wishing evil upon those who prayed with them on Sunday but beat them on Monday, tried the souls of black Christians."[21] Nevertheless, the slaves, for the most part, held to their faith, often suffering graciously, forgiving and praying for their tormenters.[22] They saw in Jesus the pattern for undeserved, redemptive suffering. They anchored their hopes to a world beyond the present, where "slave and master would stand before the throne of divine justice [and] God would balance the scales."[23]

Andrew Bryan, an eighteenth century slave preacher, was imprisoned and whipped for holding worship services in Savannah, Georgia. Bryan told the authorities "that he rejoiced not only to be whipped, but *would freely suffer death for the cause of Jesus Christ*."[24] Albert Raboteau offers other similar examples of "the holiness of American slaves" who suffered for their faith, and he includes them in the annals of the persecuted church.[25] Of them he says,

> They realized—and realized with the heart not just the head—that they were of infinite worth as children of God. The conversion experience grounded their significance in the unimpeachable authority of almighty God, no matter what white people thought and taught. They knew that they constituted ... 'a spiritual aristocracy,' ... made up of those who did not simply talk about God, but experienced His power upon the altars of their hearts.[26]

---

[21] Milton C Sernett, ed., *African American Religious History: A Documentary Witness*, 2nd ed. (Durham: Duke University Press, 1999), 6.

[22] Albert J Raboteau, "The Legacy of a Suffering Church: The Holiness of American Slaves," in *An Unbroken Circle: Linking Ancient African Christianity to the African-American Experience*, ed. Paisius Altschul (St. Louis, MO: Brotherhood of St. Moses the Black, 1997), 84.

[23] Sernett, *African American Religious History*, 6.

[24] Raboteau, "An Unbroken Circle," 77.

[25] Raboteau, "An Unbroken Circle," 74–75.

[26] Raboteau, "An Unbroken Circle," 83.

Eventually, black and white abolitionists stirred the nation's conscience over slavery's horrific injustices. But, ending slavery would cost a bloody Civil War, the bloodiest conflict in American history, pitting state against state and in some cases, members of the same family against each other. Abraham Lincoln saw "this terrible war" as divine judgment on "both North and South," specifically for the sin of slavery.[27] Julia Ward Howe's "Battle Hymn of the Republic" framed that conflict in biblical language and suggested the transforming power of Christ as the ultimate cure for injustice:

> "In the beauty of the lilies Christ was born across the sea,
> With a glory in his bosom that transfigures you and me.
> As he died to make men holy, let us die to make men free,
> While God is marching on."

However, the War and its 600,000 dead were not the only cost Whites incurred for centuries of inhumanity perpetrated on Blacks. Speaking to this issue, W.E.B. Du Bois suggested other costs: "national decadence," the "social sores" in American cities, the angry radicalism of northern Blacks, and "the enormous race complications with which God seems about to punish this nation."[28]

Beyond those visible costs, the spiritual, moral, and emotional fallout from such horrific oppression may be impossible to measure. Archbishop Desmond Tutu of South Africa refers to the "degradation into which [white persons] have fallen by dehumanizing the black person," and he expresses concern "for the liberation of the oppressor equally with that of the oppressed."[29] Du Bois observed a spiritual tie between the oppressor and the oppressed by citing John Greenleaf

---

[27] Abraham Lincoln, *Lincoln's Second Inaugural Address* (Champaign, IL: Project Gutenberg), e–book, 1, http://search.ebscohost.com/login.aspx?direct=true&scope=site&db=nlebk&db=nlabk&AN=1050200.

[28] W.E.B. Du Bois, *The Souls of Black Folk*, 16, 69, 92, 118, and 120.

[29] Desmond Tutu, "Black Theology/African Theology: Soul Mates or Antagonists?," in *Third World Liberation Theologies: A Reader*, ed. Deane William Ferm (Maryknoll, NY: Orbis Books, 1986), 262.

Whittier's line, "The slave's chains and the master's alike are broken; the one curse of the races held both in tether."[30]

Sharecropping

Emancipation, when it finally came, left most Blacks without material resources or the means of obtaining them. They walked away from the plantations with nothing more than the tattered clothes they wore. In March of 1865, Lincoln established the Freedman's Bureau to provide food and clothing for newly freed slaves and assist them in finding employment. "Chronically underfunded and understaffed, the Bureau suffered from corruption and ineffectual administration."[31]

The Lincoln administration also laid plans to provide each former slave family with land and farm implements to get a start at self-sufficiency. In fact, General William T. Sherman had issued a field order as early as January, 1865 to reserve a tract of land 30 miles wide stretching from Charleston, South Carolina to Jacksonville, Florida. This would have fulfilled the government's promise of "40 acres and a mule" for each former slave family. Regrettably, that order was rescinded when Andrew Johnson succeeded Lincoln as president.[32]

"The Civil War destroyed the economic basis of the South, and, as a result, both White and Black groped for a way to earn a livelihood from the land."[33] The sharecropping system which resulted "was generally substitution of economic slavery for their former plight. It was a rugged struggle which many did not survive."[34] William Holtzclaw, an African American educator who grew up in a sharecropper's home,

---

[30] W. E. B. Du Bois, *The Souls of Black Folk*, 1st Vintage Books/Library of America ed (New York: Vintage Books/Library of America, 1990), 59.

[31] Jemar Tisby, *The Color of Compromise: The Truth about the American Church's Complicity in Racism* (Grand Rapids, MI: Zondervan, 2019), 91.

[32] Jemar Tisby, *The Color of Compromise*, 90.

[33] Jay David, ed., *Growing up Black: From Slave Days to the Present* (New York, NY: Avon Books, 1992), 121.

[34] Jay David, ed., *Growing up Black*, 106.

describes the abuses of sharecropping. The white landlord frequently defrauded his father of wages, leaving Holtzclaw and his siblings without necessary food. Holtzclaw recalls "how at night we would often cry for food until falling here and there on the floor we would sob ourselves to sleep."[35]

The hardships of sharecropping ultimately resulted in "the great migration" during the first few decades of the twentieth century. This was the movement of six million African Americans from the rural South to northern and midwestern cities in pursuit of decent jobs, which explains the significant numbers of Blacks residing in those urban centers to this day. Sheer economic necessity forced many black men to leave their families behind while they sought better conditions for them elsewhere. Many of these families remained separated, thus continuing the decimation of black families that slavery had begun.

White Supremacy

One of the worst legacies of slavery was the doctrine of white supremacy. Martin Luther King, Jr. said, "It seems to be a fact of life that human beings cannot continue to do wrong without eventually reaching out for some rationalization to clothe their acts in the garments of righteousness. And so, with the growth of slavery, men had to convince themselves that a system which was so economically profitable was morally justifiable."[36] Some white Christians distorted the Bible to teach the inferiority of Blacks and to say that slavery functioned as God's tool to evangelize them. In time, "science" joined the chorus with elaborate but unfounded racial theories "proving" the inferiority of Blacks. As a result, even Emancipation could not free the black person from the humiliation that would ultimately crystallize in the Jim Crow system.

---

[35] William H. Holtzclaw, "From The Black Man's Burden," in *Growing Up Black: From Slave Days to the Present*, ed. Jay David, rev. (New York, NY: Avon Books, 1992), 106.

[36] King, Jr., *Where Do We Go from Here?*, location 919.

Jim Crow

Despite the privations of sharecropping, many southern Blacks began to enjoy a semblance of respectability during Reconstruction. They founded schools, opened businesses, and populated legislatures.[37] That ended in 1877 when northern Republicans capitulated to southern Democrats and KKK terrorists, pulling federal troops out of the South.[38] Southern legislatures seized the moment and crushed the rights of Blacks. The era known as Jim Crow (named for a minstrel show character) was born. It would receive constitutional endorsement with the 1896 Supreme Court case Plessy v. Ferguson, essentially making segregation the law of the land.[39]

By the turn of the twentieth century, every southern state had passed laws disenfranchising Blacks and prohibiting them from interacting with Whites in housing, jobs, restaurants, hospitals, schools, and churches. "Politicians competed with each other by proposing and passing ever more stringent, oppressive, and downright ridiculous legislation (such as laws specifically prohibiting Blacks and Whites from playing chess together)."[40] Voting laws bordering on the absurd virtually guaranteed Blacks could not vote.

There were sporadic public lynching of Blacks—often over trumped up charges or for infractions as minor as disrespecting a white person. Author Jemar Tisby describes in detail the gruesome tortures that often went along with the lynchings. Sometimes, these atrocities were staged on the grounds of black churches on Sunday afternoons "for maximum intimidation of the black populace. ... The black church has historically been the locus of religious and communal life for black people, so performing a lynching on church grounds would send a

---

[37] Michelle Alexander, *The New Jim Crow: Mass Incarceration in the Age of Colorblindness* (New York, NY: The New Press, 2012), 29.

[38] Alexander, *The New Jim Crow*, 30.

[39] Colby, *Some of My Best Friends Are Black*, location 170.

[40] Alexander, *The New Jim Crow*, 34.

message to all black people in the area that no place was safe from white power."[41] So, the Jim Crow system involved more than inconvenience and humiliation for Blacks. These random acts of terror instilled haunting fears that shadowed them day and night.

The Jim Crow system was not limited to the South. Tisby points out that "the North and West had 'sundown towns'—communities where black people had to be out before sundown or face violent repercussions. ... Towns such as Appleton, Wisconsin; Levittown on Long Island; and the Chicago suburb of Cicero, among hundreds of others, kept their communities intentionally all-white."[42] The difference was, that while these conditions existed in other parts of the country, they pervaded the South.

Bonhoeffer on Jim Crow

Some may be surprised to learn that Dietrich Bonhoeffer, the well-known German theologian martyred by the Nazis during the Holocaust, had a brush with the Jim Crow system. Bonhoeffer visited America in the 1930s to study at Union Theological Seminary in New York. His social work assignment took him to Abyssinian Baptist Church, an African American congregation in Harlem. The authentic spirituality of that church provided Bonhoeffer a welcome respite from the shallow liberalism of the seminary.[43] "Starving from the [theological] skim milk at Union, Bonhoeffer found a theological feast [at Abyssinian].[44] Pastor Adam Clayton Powell, Sr., the son of slaves, "combined the fire of a revivalist preacher with great intellect and social vision. [Powell] was active in combating racism and minced no words about the saving power of Jesus Christ."[45] Bonhoeffer "was

---

[41] Jemar Tisby, *The Color of Compromise: The Truth about the American Church's Complicity in Racism* (Grand Rapids, MI: Zondervan, 2019), 107.

[42] Tisby, 102.

[43] Eric Metaxas, *Bonhoeffer: Pastor, Martyr, Prophet, Spy: A Righteous Gentile vs. the Third Reich* (Nashville, TN: Thomas Nelson, 2010), 107.

[44] Metaxes, 108.

[45] Metaxes, 108.

entirely captivated, and for the rest of his time in New York, he was there every Sunday to worship and to teach a Sunday school class of boys."[46]

Bonhoeffer's visit also introduced him to the racial problems in America. On a trip to the South, he ran head-on into the Jim Crow system. Puzzled by the segregation and blatant racism he saw, he shared his concerns in a letter to his brother, Karl-Friedrich:

> The separation of whites from blacks in the southern states really does make a rather shameful impression. In railways that separation extends to even the tiniest details. … The way the southerners talk about the negroes is simply repugnant, and in this regard the pastors are no better than the others. … It is a bit unnerving that in a country with so inordinately many slogans about brotherhood, peace, and so on, such things still continue completely uncorrected.[47]

These experiences influenced Bonhoeffer's concern for the plight of Jews suffering under the Nazi regime in his homeland. He cut short his stay in the U.S. and returned to Germany to join the resistance against Hitler, a decision that would lead Bonhoeffer to the hangman's noose just days before the Allies took Berlin. Such is the "cost of discipleship."[48]

"Ominous Clouds of Inferiority"

The Jim Crow system would remain in effect for decades after Bonhoeffer's visit to the South. Sadly, the white church was complicit in the injustices of the times and impatient with those who called for change. In 1963, when white clergymen urged black folks to be more

---

[46] Metaxes, 108.

[47] Dietrich Bonhoeffer, *Barcelona, Berlin, New York: 1928-1931*, trans. Douglas W. Stott, vol. 10, Dietrich Bonhoeffer Works (Minneapolis, MN: Fortress Press, 2008), 269.

[48] *The Cost of Discipleship*, one of the great Christian classics of all times, is the title of Bonhoeffer's most well-known book.

patient, Martin Luther King, Jr. responded by opening a window into his personal pain over Jim Crow:

> When you suddenly find your tongue twisted and your speech stammering as you seek to explain to your six-year-old daughter why she can't go to the public amusement park that has just been advertised on television, and see tears welling up in her eyes when she is told that Funtown is closed to colored children, and see ominous clouds of inferiority beginning to form in her little mental sky, and see her beginning to distort her personality by developing an unconscious bitterness toward white people; when you have to concoct an answer for a five-year-old son who is asking: "Daddy, why do white people treat colored people so mean?"; when you take a cross-country drive and find it necessary to sleep night after night in the uncomfortable corners of your automobile because no motel will accept you; when you are humiliated day in and day out by nagging signs reading "white" and "colored"; when your first name becomes "nigger," your middle name becomes "boy" (however old you are) and your last name becomes "John," and your wife and mother are never given the respected title "Mrs."; when you are harried by day and haunted by night by the fact that you are a Negro, living constantly at tiptoe stance, never quite knowing what to expect next, and are plagued with inner fears and outer resentments; when you are forever fighting a degenerating sense of "nobodiness"—then you will understand why we find it difficult to wait.[49]

The corporate pain caused by Jim Crow eventually found righteous expression in the peaceful protests of the civil rights movement.

Civil Rights

On December 1, 1955, a Montgomery, Alabama bus driver asked Mrs. Rosa Parks, an African American woman, to relinquish her front-row seat to a white male. When she calmly refused, the police arrested her. That incident marks the beginning of the civil rights movement that would dominate American life for more than a decade and launch Martin Luther King, Jr. into national prominence. The bus boycott he organized in Montgomery ended racially segregated seating on public transportation. A year before Parks' arrest, the Supreme Court decision

---

[49] King, Jr., *Why We Can't Wait*, location 1262.

in Brown vs. the Board of Education of Topeka (KS) put a legal halt to segregated schools. Although it would not be implemented in Alabama for another ten years, Brown pulled the linchpin from Jim Crow. The Civil Rights Act of 1964 and the Voting Rights Act of 1965 dealt the death blows to legalized injustice in America.[50]

In some respects, the civil rights movement was an inevitable outcome of World War II. Nearly 900,000 African Americans in uniform had fought to liberate the world from totalitarianism. On returning to their homeland, black veterans met the same racism and discrimination they had known before the war, and long-simmering resentments boiled into open rage. King passionately felt their pain and brilliantly articulated their cause. He led his people in non-violent protests that focused the world's attention on their plight and moved the federal government to implement sweeping societal changes.

Not only was King a powerful advocate for justice for the black community, the white community owes him a debt of gratitude for saving America from the horrors of an all-out race war. Recalling his brush with death when a deranged woman plunged a knife into his chest, missing his aorta by a hair, King said, "In the summer of 1963 the knife of violence was just that close to the nation's aorta."[51] He explained that racial tensions would have plunged hundreds of cities into violence that year, costing countless lives, if not for the commitment to non-violence in the leaders of the civil rights movement.

Many are aware that Mahatma Gandhi of India was a source of King's doctrine of non-violent resistance. But few realize that King's most important source for this was Jesus. A life-long friend of King's father, Howard Thurman, wrote a book titled *Jesus and the Disinherited*, a book

---

[50] Harry R. Jackson, Jr., *The Truth in Black & White* (Lake Mary, FL: FrontLine, 2008), 192.

[51] King, Jr., *Why We Can't Wait*, location 188.

that King often carried in his travels.[52] That book presents Jesus, the suffering Jew, acquainted with poverty and under the oppressive regime of Rome, as the perfect model for all oppressed people.[53] According to Thurman, Jesus taught that "hatred is destructive to hated and hater alike."[54] It would be accurate to say, then, that King found in Jesus the greatest example for non-violent resistance to, and love for, one's enemies.

Even from the early days of the Montgomery bus boycott, King framed the issues within a Christian context. Addressing the Montgomery Improvement Association, the precursor to his Southern Christian Leadership Conference (SCLC), King said,

> We have before us the glorious opportunity to inject a new dimension of love into the veins of our civilization. There is still a voice crying out in terms that echo across the generations, saying: "Love your enemies, bless them that curse you, pray for them that despitefully use you, that you may be the children of your Father which is in Heaven."[55]

The goal King had in mind far exceeded the immediate gains of the boycott: "The end is reconciliation, the end is redemption ... the end is the creation of the beloved community."[56]

Charles Marsh laments that some "historians and scholars have recast the civil rights movement as a secular movement that used religion to its advantage."[57] They are dead wrong. Historian Paul Harvey insists that "Black Christians formed the rank and file of the Civil Rights Movement. ... The civil rights revolution in American history was, to a considerable degree, a religious revolution."[58]

---

[52] Howard Thurman, *Jesus and the Disinherited*, Kindle e-book, location 62.

[53] Thurman, location 28.

[54] Thurman, location 35.

[55] Marsh, *The Beloved Community*, Kindle e–book, location 60.

[56] Marsh, location 60.

[57] Marsh, location 120.

[58] Harvey, "Religion, Civil Rights, and Social Justice," Kindle e–book, 496–97.

"I Heard the Voice of Jesus"

King's writings underscore the spiritual and religious thrust behind the movement. One example of this came immediately following the success of the Montgomery bus boycott. King received a threatening phone call late one night after his family had gone to bed. Unable to sleep, he heated a pot of coffee and sat down at his kitchen table. With his face in his hands, he cried out to God in utter desperation, confessing his fear and discouragement. He later recalled the moment:

> It seemed as though I could hear the quiet assurance of an inner voice saying: "Martin Luther, stand up for righteousness. Stand up for justice. Stand up for truth. And lo, I will be with you. Even until the end of the world." I tell you I've seen the lightning flash. I've heard the thunder roar. I've felt sin breakers dashing trying to conquer my soul. But I heard the voice of Jesus saying still to fight on. He promised never to leave me alone. At that moment I experienced the presence of the Divine as I had never experienced Him before. Almost at once my fears began to go. My uncertainty disappeared. I was ready to face anything.[59]

A few days later, King's newfound courage encountered a major test when segregationists bombed his house. Away at a meeting when he heard the news, he ran home to check on his wife and baby daughter. A crowd of sympathetic neighbors had already gathered in his front yard, some of them armed and calling for retaliation. But King challenged the angry crowd from his front porch:

> We believe in law and order. Don't get panicky. ... Don't get your weapons. He who lives by the sword will perish by the sword. Remember that is what God said. We are not advocating violence. We want to love our enemies. I want you to love our enemies. Be good to them. Love them and let them know you love them. ... For what we are doing is right. What we are doing is just. And God is with us.[60]

King often found himself in a tug of war between two powerful opposing forces—white segregationists on the one hand, and black nationalists on the other—both of them advocating violence. Indeed,

---

[59] Clayborne Carson, *The Autobiography of Martin Luther King, Jr.*, 78.
[60] Clayborne Carson, 80.

in 1963 some black nationalists were calling for "a colossal bloodbath to cleanse the nation's sins."[61] Malcolm X, a contemporary of King, saw in the Declaration of Independence "a model for violent upheaval" against oppression.[62] Although Malcolm never advocated outright armed aggression, he encouraged Blacks to arm themselves for self-defense. Ultimately, even leaders of the Student Nonviolent Coordinating Committee (SNCC) abandoned their Christian nonviolent appeals in favor of a militant black nationalism strikingly similar to that of Malcolm X."[63]

King expressed "patience and understanding" with those who espoused such views, because "for twelve years I ... had held out radiant promises of progress. ... Their hopes had soared. They were now booing because they felt that we were unable to deliver on our promises."[64] Nevertheless, King also understood the flaw in their reasoning. "[The Black Power movement] rejects the one thing that keeps the fire of revolutions burning: the ever-present flame of hope. When hope dies, a revolution degenerates into an undiscriminating catchall for evanescent and futile gestures."[65]

King continued to argue that "non-violence is a powerful and just weapon. It is a weapon unique in history which cuts without wounding and ennobles the man who wields it. It is a sword that heals."[66] One wonders how many Americans appreciate the enormous debt they owe King for preventing countless deaths, or how many appreciate the tragic irony of his untimely death at the hands of violent men.

---

[61] King, Jr., *Why We Can't Wait*, location 471.
[62] Miller, "Plymouth Rock Landed On Us," 211.
[63] Miller, "Plymouth Rock Landed On Us," 212.
[64] King, Jr., *Where Do We Go from Here?*, Kindle e–book, 46.
[65] King, Jr., *Where Do We Go from Here?*, Kindle e–book, 47.
[66] King, Jr., *Why We Can't Wait*, location 327.

Backlash

Sadly, King's insistence on non-violent protest was met with an ugly segregationist backlash. Feeling their way of life threatened, some in the white community reacted to non-violence with police brutality and government-sanctioned violence. Images of police dogs attacking protesters and water cannons knocking them to the streets filled the news. Activists were beaten and murdered; homes and churches were bombed; and more often than not, such crimes went unsolved. On a Sunday morning in September, 1963, a bomb exploded in the Sunday School of the Sixteenth Street Baptist Church in Birmingham, Alabama, killing four little girls. King later recalled the events of that day and the days that followed:

> These were terrible deeds but they are strangely less terrible than the response of the dominant white community. ... Perhaps the poverty of conscience of the white majority was most clearly illustrated at the funeral of the child martyrs. No white official attended. No white faces could be seen save for a pathetically few courageous ministers. More than children were buried that day; honor and decency were also interred.[67]

More terrible than the halting response of the white community was the dismal failure of white Evangelicals to read the signs of the times and join their black brothers and sisters in the quest for justice. Considering the fact that more than a hundred years earlier, white Christians *founded and led* the Abolitionist movement, the failure of white Christians at this strategic juncture is all the more tragic.

The Lost Legacy of White Evangelicals

In April of 1963, Birmingham authorities placed King in solitary confinement in the city jail. The next morning someone slid a newspaper under his cell door. Examining it, King saw an ad taken out by eight white clergymen criticizing his tactics and calling for an end to the protests. Grieved by this, King responded with an open letter.

---

[67] King, Jr., *Why We Can't Wait*, location 1791.

Having nothing but the newspaper to write on, he scribbled his thoughts along its margins, then on scraps of paper slipped to him by a prison trustee. Known as "Letter from Birmingham Jail," the treatise contains one of King's most profound arguments for the righteousness of non-violent protest. In it, he poignantly expressed his disappointment over the white church's failure to support the cause of justice:

> When I was suddenly catapulted into the leadership of the bus protest in Montgomery, Alabama, a few years ago, I felt we would be supported by the white church. I felt that the white ministers ... of the South would be among our strongest allies. Instead, some have been outright opponents, refusing to understand the freedom movement and misrepresenting its leaders; all too many others have been more cautious than courageous and have remained silent behind the anesthetizing security of stained-glass windows. ... In deep disappointment I have wept over the laxity of the Church. ... There was a time when the Church was very powerful—in the time when the early Christians rejoiced at being deemed worthy to suffer for what they believed. ... Things are different now. So often the contemporary Church is a weak, ineffectual voice with an uncertain sound. So often it is an arch-defender of the status quo. ... If today's Church does not recapture the sacrificial spirit of the early Church, it will lose its authenticity, forfeit the loyalty of millions, and be dismissed as an irrelevant social club with no meaning for the twentieth century.[68]

Considering the way today's culture has marginalized the Church, King's words were prophetic. The anti-Christian bias in today's society and black Christians' support of secularist politicians may be the harvest of seeds sown in the past. Bishop Harry R. Jackson, Jr. observes,

> Fifty years ago, the national evangelical movement missed a great opportunity to help direct the civil rights movement. If the white church in the South had preached against racism and called for local churches to lead the movement for justice on biblical grounds, they could have helped navigate the nation through many strife-filled years.[69]

---

[68] Clayborne Carson, ed., *The Autobiography of Martin Luther King, Jr.* (New York, NY: Warner Books, 1998), 199–201.

[69] Jackson, Jr., *The Truth in Black & White*, 213.

Jackson believes "the desertion of the Christian Right from the struggle" explains why King and other civil rights activists welcomed liberal churchmen and secularist politicians into the movement. "In the absence of … the moral base that is the natural home for most Blacks, they opened the door for politically active Blacks to be seduced by the Left. Blacks were looking for acceptance, and the presence of Whites marching beside them in the face of police brutality was a public validation."[70]

One thing we must bear in mind in this discussion, is that those Evangelicals did not have the benefit of our current perspective. Since their time, we have experienced decades of societal changes that have educated us in race relations far beyond anything they understood. It's wrong to judge that generation by the same standard we use in judging the current generation. I say this, not to excuse them, but to avoid becoming self-righteous in my condemnation of them. The fact is, most of us are products of our times rather than prophets to our times. That being said, the absence of Evangelicals from the civil rights movement explains, to some extent, the widening political gap between Whites and Blacks—a topic we will explore in depth in Chapter Seven.

"Fragmentation and Disillusionment"

Following King's assassination, the civil rights movement floundered for a variety of reasons, the first being a vacuum of leadership. Although his able associate, Ralph David Abernathy, became head of the SCLC, no one could fill King's shoes. He was a leader for his times without equal. Beyond that, student protests and the Viet Nam War displaced the movement in the national news and siphoned away federal funds. Tangent movements like the Black Panthers and Black Muslims challenged the goals of the movement and diminished its force. The departure from its Christian moorings, as it courted an

---

[70] Jackson, Jr. *The Truth in Black & White,* 195.

increasingly secularist political establishment, also hurt the movement. Marsh says, "The story of the civil rights movement in America concludes with this final period of fragmentation and disillusionment."[71]

The Pentecostal Movement: A Divine Strategy?

There are some bright spots in this otherwise gloomy portrait of the evangelical church, but even bright spots can have their shadows. The pentecostal outpouring at the turn of the twentieth century is a case in point. This movement that arose from Methodist and Holiness roots, gave prominence to the person and work of the Holy Spirit and restored to the Church the supernatural sign-gifts that grace the pages of the book of Acts. Evidence suggests that God may have intended even more for the pentecostal movement, which, from its inception, was multi-racial.

Many cite the Azusa Street revival of 1906 as the beginning of modern-day Pentecostalism. The revival was led by an African American pastor named William Seymour, whose congregation met in a former livery stable on Azusa Street in Los Angeles, California. As word of the spiritual outpouring spread, people of every ethnicity and nationality were drawn to the humble facility, and Seymour welcomed them. The press took notice and publicized the revival, reporting the unusual manifestations of the Spirit and the integrated gatherings. Almost incredibly, well-to-do Whites mingled happily with the poorest Blacks, as both were captivated by the love of God that flowed freely in the services. In the decades that followed, the movement would grow into a multi-racial, world-wide phenomenon.

Azusa happened during the peak of the Jim Crow era, so this mixing of the races scandalized many. However, others rejoiced to see Blacks and Whites worshiping and praying together, embracing one another

---

[71] Marsh, *The Beloved Community*, location 136.

as brothers and sisters in the same family. Frank Bartleman, the chronicler of the revival famously "exulted that at 'Old Azusa ... the color line' had been 'washed away in the blood.'"[72] Roswith Gerloff muses that "one may draw the conclusion that Pentecostalism did not just accidentally arise at the threshold of a century so full of racism [and] oppression."[73]

Is it possible that the pentecostal movement was a divine strategy to change the racial dynamics in twentieth century America? In the words of Cecil M. Robeck, Jr.,

> [T]he Azusa Street Mission provides a glimpse of what is possible if we allow space for the Holy Spirit to change hearts and minds. It may also provide a model for congregations in our own day to embrace this same kind of diversity, to demonstrate before the world the power of the gospel to break down the artificial racial and ethnic walls that otherwise divide us.[74]

Regrettably, the interracial unity that began at Azusa was short-lived. Although God's ultimate plan for the Church will prevail, the human element often causes setbacks and delays. Within a couple of years, the revival dissipated as factions and racial tensions splintered the leadership. Eventually, the burgeoning movement that grew from Azusa Street succumbed to the pressure of the wider culture and became segregated. The forces that produced the Jim Crow system in the first place were also at work in many Pentecostals. Instead of the Church changing the culture, once again, the culture changed the Church.

---

[72] Edith Blumhofer, "Revisiting Azusa Street: A Centennial Retrospect," *International Bulletin of Missionary Research* 30, no. 2 (April 1, 2006): 61.

[73] Gerloff wrote the forward to Leonard Lovett's *Kingdom Beyond Color: Re-Examining the Phenomenon of Racism* (Xlibris, 2009), Kindle e–book, location 50.

[74] Cecil M. Robeck, Jr., *Azusa Street Mission and Revival: The Birth of the Global Pentecostal Movement* (Nashville, TN: Thomas Nelson, Inc., 2006) 14.

In 1939 the Assemblies of God (AG), the largest white pentecostal group, officially disapproved the ordaining of black ministers,[75] and in 1948 they helped form the Pentecostal Fellowship of North America (PFNA), an association of white pentecostal denominations. No effort was made to include their African American sister churches, such as the Church of God in Christ (COGIC) in the association. Darrin Rodgers, the historian of the Assemblies of God, laments that pentecostal people "have been subject to the same cultural confusion and prejudices that have afflicted those in the society around them."[76]

"Miracle in Memphis"

But God did not abandon these "people of the Spirit." Just as He pushed the early church toward racial inclusiveness, the Holy Spirit has been leading Pentecostals on a journey to reconciliation. In 1989, the AG passed a resolution opposing "the sin of racism in any form," and calling for its members to repent, work against racism, and seek reconciliation.[77]

Another significant milestone involved a 1994 gathering in Memphis, Tennessee. Three thousand people representing PFNA denominations, African American denominations, and charismatic groups gathered in the city where King had been assassinated, and where the mother church of COGIC was located. During the sessions, white leaders presented papers acknowledging culpability for their sins of prejudice and injustice.

In the afternoon session on October 18, the conference agenda was unexpectedly side-lined by unplanned expressions from the audience. There was a message in tongues, after which pastor Jack Hayford gave

---

[75] Lois Olena, "I'm Sorry, My Brother," in *We've Come This Far: Reflections on the Pentecostal Tradition and Racial Reconciliation*, ed. Byron D. Klaus (Springfield, MO: Assemblies of God Theological Seminary, 2007), 131.

[76] Darrin J. Rodgers, "The Assemblies of God and the Long Journey toward Racial Reconciliation," *Assemblies of God Heritage* 28 (2008): 58.

[77] Assemblies of God, "Minutes of the 1989 General Council," n.d., 117–18.

an impassioned interpretation. Suddenly, a white pastor appeared on stage with a bottle of water and proceeded to wash the feet of Bishop Clemmons of COGIC, all the while begging forgiveness for the sins of his people against his black brothers and sisters. Then Bishop Blake, an African American, washed the feet of AG superintendent Thomas Trask. With tears in his eyes, Blake entreated his fellow delegates: "Brothers and sisters, I commit my love to you. There are problems down the road, but a strong commitment to love will overcome them."[78]

These unscripted events moved the entire audience to tears and other visible emotional responses that seemed to confirm God's approval on the meetings. The next day pastor Paul Walker of the Church of God, called the event "the Miracle in Memphis," a term that has identified the conference ever since.[79] Before the conference ended, the participants disbanded the PFNA and formed a new, racially inclusive organization: Pentecostal/Charismatic Churches of North America. Significantly, the first leader of the new organization was the presiding bishop of COGIC.[80]

The following year, the AG passed a resolution calling for greater inclusion of black ministers. In it they confessed, "Our testimony to the world has suffered as a result of this separation and our fellowship has been deprived of the rich blessings which could have been made by our black brothers and sisters."[81] Later, they undertook other steps that resulted in the racial expansion of the AG constituency. "Since membership follows leadership, it is no accident that, in 2006, 35% of

---

[78] Synan, "Memphis 1994: Miracle and Mandate," 16.

[79] Synan, 14.

[80] DeYoung, "The Wiley-Blackwell Companion to Religion and Social Justice," Kindle e–book, 70.

[81] Byron D. Klaus, ed., "Resolution 25 Revised. Use of Black Ministers," in *We've Come This Far: Reflections on the Pentecostal Tradition and Racial Reconciliation* (Springfield, MO: Assemblies of God Theological Seminary, 2007), 116.

US Assemblies of God adherents were non-Anglo."[82] (Since then, that number has risen to 40%.) The crowning moment in this remarkable sequence occurred in 2007 when Zollie Smith was elected Director of US Missions, the first African American to serve as an executive officer of the Assemblies of God.

Today, more than 600 million believers around the world identify as Pentecostals or Charismatics, and the movement retains the multi-ethnic and multi-national flavor it acquired at Azusa Street. Overall, Pentecostals are more urban than rural, more female than male, more Two-Thirds world than Western, more impoverished than affluent, and younger than eighteen.[83] Like the first Pentecost described in the book of Acts, this modern-day phenomenon is evidence of God's favor on racial inclusiveness in His Church.

Pentecostals are not alone in repenting of past racism. Other evangelical groups, such as the Southern Baptists, have also issued formal statements of repentance for such failures. Unfortunately, these efforts, while praiseworthy, came too late to influence the course of the civil rights movement and its leaders. We must conclude that if God's purpose was to use the pentecostal movement to heal racial division in America during the twentieth century, the movement fell short of that ideal. The century ended with racial division still a significant factor in American life.

~~~~~~~~~~~

[82] Rodgers, "The Assemblies of God and the Long Journey toward Racial Reconciliation," 59. According to George O. Wood in an email dated February 14, 2014, "More than 40 percent of the current [AG] membership in the United States is made up of ethnic minorities."

[83] L. Grant McClung, Jr., "'Try to Get People Saved': Revisiting the Paradigm of an Urgent Pentecostal Missiology," in *The Globalization of Pentecostalism: A Religion Made to Travel*, ed. Murray W. Dempster, Byron D. Klaus, and Douglas Peterson (Cowan, CA: Regnum Books International, 1999), 47.

The civil rights movement accomplished much in the quest for justice and racial equality and laid the foundation for reconciliation, healing, and harmony. Nevertheless, much remains to be accomplished. If we are to build on that foundation, we must open our eyes to the ongoing challenges of corporate pain, racial insensitivity, and racialization, the subject of the next chapter.

6

PRESENT CHALLENGES:
Corporate Pain and Racialization

"Blacks fall below the poverty line more than three times as often as non-Hispanic Whites, and they are far less likely to own their own homes than white Americans. Furthermore, their median household wealth is 8 percent of that of Whites." [1]

In the previous chapter, we took an honest and painful look at American history, and learned that Whites and Blacks perceive that history very differently, because their experiences with it are very different. We also discussed the important gains of the civil rights movement, which undeniably changed the trajectory of American history where race is concerned.

The problem is, many white people tend to flatter the civil rights movement far too much, seeing it as the historic "cure-all" for the nation's race problems. In their minds, "problem solved, let's move on." As a result, Whites are often frustrated when Blacks don't seem to appreciate those gains, and instead, continue to "play the race card." To many white people, black people still carry a "chip on the shoulder."

Our effort to understand one another at this juncture calls for another honest and painful look—this time, at the present situation in America where race is concerned. Here's where the journey gets a little dicey. I expect that both Whites and Blacks will disagree with some things I

---

[1] Emerson and Smith, *Divided by Faith*, location 1946.

say in this chapter. Even if you disagree, remember this: what is essential to *koinonia* is not agreeing with each other, but understanding each other. In the following paragraphs, I'm not trying to "convert" you to either position. I'm simply asking you to read with an open mind and, more importantly, an open heart. Besides, even if you disagree with some of my statements, I think you will agree with my final analysis. If you find you just can't wade through some of this, before you leave the chapter, be sure to read my closing story about "a spiritual earthquake" that occurred in Jasper County, Texas. It will touch your heart.

Our effort to understand one another calls for a willingness to consider some of the ongoing fallout of our painful history: things like corporate pain, racial insensitivity, and racialization. Don't worry if those terms don't resonate. We're going to explore and explain each of them.

Corporate Pain

In chapter four we considered the cultural differences between Whites and Blacks and the fact that we view life through six different cultural lenses. We learned that one of those lenses is "the source of identity" lens. This has to do with whether we think individually or corporately. Let me say it this way: in general, white people tend to think of themselves as individuals, and black people tend to identify with their community. Argentine Evangelist Ed Silvoso observes that "white folks are one of the few people-groups who do not have a people-group mentality."[2] On the other hand, many African Americans view reality through their "people-group mentality."

Martin Luther King, Jr. acknowledged this corporate mindset in the black community:

> Negroes are almost instinctively cohesive. We band together readily, and against white hostility we have an intense and wholesome loyalty to each

---

[2] Ed Silvoso, *Prayer Evangelism: How to Change the Spiritual Climate over Your Home, Neighborhood, and City* (Ventura, CA: Regal Books, 2000), Kindle e-book, 137.

other. In some of the simplest relationships we will protect a brother even at a cost to ourselves. We are loath to be witnesses against each other when the white man seeks to divide us. We are acutely conscious of the need and sharply sensitive to the importance of defending our own. Solidarity is a reality in Negro life, as it always has been among the oppressed."[3]

Not every black person today would agree with King on this point—especially as it relates to current attitudes. I have talked to some African Americans who see the corporate mindset as perhaps true of the past, but not so much today. Nevertheless, King's comment introduces the concept of "corporate pain,"[4] something Black theologian James H. Cone described as "the pain of being black in a white racist society."[5] Understanding this concept can help explain the eruptions in the African American community over perceptions of blatant injustice against one of their own.

The Rodney King beating demonstrates this point. In 1991, when white policemen subdued and beat Rodney King during a routine traffic stop, a video of the incident made national news and evoked divergent reactions. "To whites, the incident represented an issue between individuals: Rodney King and the officers who beat him. African-Americans reacted quite differently. What they registered was the beating of the black race by the white race."[6] John Dawson adds, "The actions of a handful of people on March 3, 1991, touched a vast bruise in the American soul and set off a shock wave of protest, violence and looting that took 59 lives … and triggered riots in major cities from coast to coast."[7] For African Americans, the not-guilty verdict in the trial of the four white police officers conjured too many memories of injustice from their corporate history. The psychic pain

---

[3] King, Jr., *Where Do We Go from Here?*, location 1856.

[4] Patterson, *Bridging the Racial and Political Divide*, 35.

[5] Cone, *A Black Theology of Liberation*, 5.

[6] Silvoso, *Prayer Evangelism*, Kindle e–book, 137.

[7] John Dawson, *Healing America's Wounds* (Ventura, CA: Regal Books, 1994), 20.

and suppressed rage over centuries of racism boiled to the surface, overwhelming human capacity to restrain it.

Corporate pain also explains the "chip on the shoulder" attitude that some Whites occasionally perceive in some Blacks. Viewed against the backdrop of a lifetime of discrimination and countless humiliations, however, the "chip" is entirely understandable. Archbishop Desmond Tutu spoke of the humiliation he experienced as a Black in South Africa. Describing the "iniquitous pass law system" imposed on Blacks under Apartheid, Tutu said, "It was not usually the big things, the awful atrocities, that got at you. No, it was the daily pinpricks, the little discourtesies, the minute humiliations, having one's dignity trodden underfoot, not always with jackboots—though that happened too."[8]

Racial Insensitivity

I may lose some of my white readers at this point, although I hope not. I hope they can track with me through this section, painful as it may be. Because, whether we acknowledge it or not, racial insensitivity among Whites compounds the corporate pain of Blacks. The term "racial insensitivity" refers to the fact that many Whites come across as dismissive of the past sufferings and present sensibilities of Blacks. In fact, surveys suggest that Whites respond impatiently to what they perceive as a "chip on the shoulder" attitude in Blacks.[9]

Recall with me our conversation about cultural differences in chapter four and what Patty Lane calls the "temporal lens"—the way we view time. Westerners view time as limited, segmented, and precisely measured, while most of the world sees time as abundant, flexible, and historical. Patty Lane says, "In the historical view of time, one's history is always present in the now." This explains, to some extent, why black

---

[8] Desmond Tutu, *No Future without Forgiveness* (New York, NY: Doubleday, 2000), 96.

[9] Michael O. Emerson and Christian Smith, *Divided by Faith: Evangelical Religion and the Problem of Race in America* (Oxford; New York: Oxford University Press, 2000), Kindle e-book, locations 1716–45.

people find it difficult to let go of their past. Their past is part and parcel of who they are now.

White people, on the other hand, have less of a problem forgetting their past. For example, white people tend to see slavery as a sin of their ancestors, but one for which they bear no present responsibility. Silvoso challenges this in rather strong words: "White folks absolve themselves [of the sin of slavery] individually, but they stand condemned corporately, even though they may have difficulty seeing it this way."[10]

Of course, many white people would challenge Silvoso's statement. And there's the rub: Blacks and Whites often see this situation differently, because they view all of life through different cultural lenses. And our lenses color what we see.

The solution to this dilemma is not to persuade the other side that our side is right. That will never happen, because the argument is unwinnable. The solution is to LISTEN to each other with an open mind. The solution is to try to UNDERSTAND how the other side views the issues, seeking to EMPATHIZE with the pain many of our fellow human beings bear. How else can we have a reasonable conversation with each other about these issues?

All too often, listening, understanding, and empathy are lacking in our conversations about race, which translates into racial insensitivity. Let me give you some examples.

Sociologists Michael Emerson and Christian Smith conducted interviews with many white Evangelicals to determine their racial sensitivity. A sampling of responses includes the following. (Bear in mind, these are statements by white *Christians*):

---

[10] Ed Silvoso, *Prayer Evangelism: How to Change the Spiritual Climate over Your Home, Neighborhood, and City* (Ventura, CA: Regal Books, 2000), Kindle e–book, 137.

"We need to forget the past; we can't undo it. We have to go forward. I think a lot of people are expecting restitution for something this society had nothing to do with."

"I believe there are Blacks that hold a grudge about slavery still. None of us that are alive today, first of all, were alive then. So don't hold it against me for something that happened years and years ago."

"The black race, they need to let go of their roots that their great-great-great-great-grandfather was persecuted as a slave. So be it. That was wrong, but we're living now."[11]

Racial insensitivity does not always manifest itself this overtly. More often it comes in the form of attitudes about economic disparity and its causes, as well as government programs to level the playing field. According to Pew Research, "One of the defining values gaps between Blacks and Whites is over opportunity. Currently, half of Blacks say 'success in life is determined by forces outside our control,' compared with 31% of Whites."[12] Similarly, 61 percent of Blacks see little real improvement in the African American situation in this country. Only 33 percent of Whites agree.[13]

This brings us to the subject of racialization. Scott Williams, a Black pastor, says, "We live in an incredibly racialized culture and most White folks are oblivious to that reality and painfully ignorant on issues of race. The Church in general is embarrassingly ignorant on race, and much less does it have a biblical theology of race."[14]

---

[11] Michael O. Emerson and Christian Smith, *Divided by Faith: Evangelical Religion and the Problem of Race in America*, locations 1724–34.

[12] *Partisan Polarization Surges in Bush, Obama Years*, Trends in American Values 1987-2012 (Washington, DC: The Pew Research Center for the People and the Press, June 4, 2012), 97, http://www.people-press.org/files/legacy-pdf/06-04-12%20Values%20Release.pdf., 31.

[13] *Partisan Polarization*, 87.

[14] Scott Williams, *Church Diversity: Sunday the Most Segregated Day of the Week* (Green Forest, AR: New Leaf Press, 2011), Kindle e–book, location 2274.

Racialization

Emerson and Smith use the term "racialization" to describe the present state of life in post-Civil Rights America. Not to be confused with the word "racism," the term "racialization" refers primarily to the ongoing economic disparity between Whites and Blacks in America. "A racialized society is a society wherein race matters profoundly for differences in life experiences, life opportunities, and social relationships."[15] In other words, even though racial discrimination has been officially outlawed, huge disparities persist in the economic and social rewards that accrue to Whites and Blacks. Tanner Colby offers an example:

> In my generation more Blacks have graduated from college than at any other time in history, yet the social, cultural, and economic gaps persist. The unemployment rate for black college grads is double that of white college grads. Rich/poor, North/South, red state/blue state, the color line seems to follow us everywhere.[16]

Consider these facts: Blacks fall below the poverty line more than three times as often as non-Hispanic Whites, and they are far less likely to own their own homes. According to Emerson and Smith, the median household wealth of Blacks is 8 percent of that of Whites,[17] and that disparity doesn't appear to be lessening. A later study revealed that "a typical white household has sixteen times the wealth of a black one. ... [Furthermore,] black people comprise about 13 percent of the population but hold less than 3 percent of the nation's total wealth."[18] To quote an African American friend of mine, "We feel we have to work twice as hard to get half as much."

You may be surprised that such disparities still exist so long after civil rights. These realities often lie beneath the surface of our conscious awareness, and we just don't see them, unless someone points them

---

[15] Emerson and Smith, *Divided by Faith*, location 175.

[16] Colby, *Some of My Best Friends Are Black*, locations 141–51.

[17] Emerson and Smith, *Divided by Faith*, location 1946.

[18] Jemar Tisby, *The Color of Compromise*, 198.

out. Professor Johan Mostert, a white man, explains why Whites don't see certain aspects of society. Before you read his statement, let me warn you that he uses a term that causes many white people to bristle. Instead of bristling, try to understand his point. This is what he says: "White privilege ... operates outside the level of conscious awareness" constituting an "invisible veil" that blinds Whites to the "advantages they cash in each day."[19] In other words, because white people are white, they can't fully appreciate what it is like *not* to be white. We are accustomed to life as we know it, and we live unaware of the unearned assets that accrue to us simply because we belong to the dominant culture.

(Again, I am speaking in general terms. Many Blacks have risen out of poverty and enjoy material benefits unknown to some Whites who remain bound in generational poverty. I do not mean to minimize anyone's suffering.)

Back to the topic. Even for those who acknowledge these racial disparities, they often misattribute their cause. According to Emerson and Smith, the protestant work ethic and rugged individualism of white Evangelicals skew their perception of the African American plight, causing them to see it as an individual or cultural problem, rather than a structural or systemic problem. For example, many Whites believe the gains of the civil rights movement completely leveled the playing field, and economic gaps persist because African Americans do not try hard enough.

Most Blacks strongly disagree. Martin Luther King, Jr. warned of the danger that these disparities would be attributed "to innate Negro weaknesses and used to justify further neglect and to rationalize continued oppression."[20] Using more colorful words, King said, "When [the Black man] seeks opportunity, he is told, in effect, to lift

---

[19] Johan Mostert, "Global and Community Leadership," Core 3 Course at Assemblies of God Theological Seminary, Springfield, MO, June 7, 2011.

[20] King, Jr., *Where Do We Go from Here?*, location 1319.

himself by his own bootstraps, advice which does not take into account the fact that he is barefoot."[21]

Consider, for example, that enslaved black people, laboring for centuries without pay and without property ownership, had no way to accumulate wealth and therefore, no wealth to transmit to their children. Later generations of Blacks who worked for pay under the inequities of Jim Crow, were limited to menial jobs at minimal pay. This is one reason many African Americans today are off to a slow start in the economic race.

But injustice is not confined to the past. Jemar Tisby suggests more current reasons for the economic gap between Whites and Blacks: "Redlining in real estate, denying bank loans to people of color, and higher unemployment rates among black people."[22]

A fair treatment of this subject calls for a look at other systemic causes of the economic disparity between Whites and Blacks. Much has been written about the damaging impact Lyndon Johnson's "War on Poverty" has had on the black family. Policies that governed Johnson's programs contributed to the disintegration of the black family by discouraging marriage, and statistics show that marriage is an essential component of financial stability in all families. According to Kay Hymowitz, "Almost 70 percent of black children are born to single mothers. Those mothers are far more likely than married mothers to be poor. ... They are also more likely to pass that poverty on to their children."[23] Remarkably, the evidence suggests that black families with both a father and a mother in the home, today earn higher incomes than their white counterparts, on average.

---

[21] King, Jr., *Why We Can't Wait*, location 288.

[22] Jemar Tisby, *The Color of Compromise*, 198.

[23] Kay Hymowitz, "The Black Family: 40 Years of Lies," *City Journal Magazine*, Summer 2005, https://www.city-journal.org/html/black-family-40-years-lies-12872.html.

The dismantling of the black nuclear family can be traced to the 1960s, when President Johnson launched his 'war'. Christopher Arps, a member of the Project 21 Black Leadership Network, laments:

> Roughly 75 percent of black children were born to a married two-parent family when the [War on Poverty] began in 1964. By 2008, the percentage of black babies born out of wedlock numbered over 72 percent. Today, the rate of unwed motherhood in the black community is more than twice as high as among whites—and almost three times higher than before big government's grand intervention.[24]

Solutions?

Blacks and Whites not only disagree about the cause of the economic gap, they also disagree about its solution. For example, Blacks and Whites hold "starkly different" opinions on programs like Affirmative Action. According to Pew Research, 62 percent of Blacks said that "every possible effort should be made, including the use of preferential treatment, to improve conditions for minorities." On the same survey, only 22 percent of Whites agreed.[25]

Most Blacks believe the solution to poverty lies in changing economic structures through government policies and programs. Considering the economic slow start given to most Blacks in American society, their view holds merit. In the nineteenth century, the American government gave land in the west to white European immigrants to provide them an "economic floor."[26] In the twentieth century, the government gave $20,000 to each Japanese-American confined to internment camps during World War II, along with an official apology.[27]

Remarkably, freed slaves did not receive such consideration after the Civil War. With this in mind, King lobbied the American government

---

[24] Project 21 Press Release, "LBJ's 'War on Poverty' Hurt Black Americans," January 8, 2014 https://nationalcenter.org/project21/2014/01/08/lbjs-war-on-poverty-hurt-black-americans/

[25] *Partisan Polarization*, 89.

[26] King, Jr., *Where Do We Go from Here?*, location 997.

[27] Jemar Tisby, *The Color of Compromise*, 199.

(unsuccessfully) to provide a minimum annual income for poor Blacks. Note the pathos in his appeal:

> Four million newly liberated slaves found themselves with no bread to eat, no land to cultivate, no shelter to cover their heads. It was like freeing a man who had been unjustly imprisoned for years, and on discovering his innocence sending him out with no bus fare to get home, no suit to cover his body, no financial compensation to atone for his long years of incarceration and to help him get a sound footing in society; sending him out with only the assertion: "Now you are free." What greater injustice could society perpetrate?[28]

Uncle Sam's Plantation

On the other hand, other voices in the African American community warn of the danger of looking to the government as provider. And, at this point, I may lose some of my black readers, although I hope not. I hope you will track with me through the next couple of paragraphs, even if you do not agree. I share this information respectfully.

Star Parker, the founder of the Center for Urban Renewal and Education (CURE) says, "the federal government has replaced religion as the answer for people in need."[29] Referring to government welfare as "Uncle Sam's Plantation," she says it deceives the poor about the destructive consequences of their choices[30] and undermines black families.[31] What makes these comments all the more remarkable is that Star Parker is an African American.

Similarly, Pastor M.L. Johnson, also African American, cautions that "liberalism is actually a system based upon control, not compassion."[32] Bishop Harry Jackson, another Black who challenges the dependency mindset, says, "More often than not, big government programs turn

---

[28] King, Jr., *Where Do We Go from Here?*, location 988.

[29] Parker, *Uncle Sam's Plantation*, 72.

[30] Parker, 91–92.

[31] Parker, 99.

[32] Melvin L Johnson, *Overcoming Racism... through the Gospel* (Longwood, FL: Xulon Press, 2007), 160.

out to be big disappointments."[33] While acknowledging the occasional need for government assistance, Jackson calls for the present generation of Blacks to "take responsibility for its own success."[34]

Indeed, a growing number of black entrepreneurs and professionals are demonstrating the rewards of effort and determination. Dr. Ben Carson, a black pediatric neurosurgeon, exemplifies this success. Raised in poverty by a single mother, he achieved success through discipline, determination, and a robust faith in God. Carson warns of the dangers of over-dependence on the government: "Our founders fully realized that prolonged government-sponsored charity would destroy the values of hard work, self-reliance, and compassion."[35]

This is not to suggest that African Americans who have not achieved Carson's success were not disciplined or determined. Nor does Carson argue against government assistance for the poor. In fact, as one who benefited from government assistance, he takes a balanced approach, calling for the allocation of "significant resources ... providing education and opportunity for the poor."[36] Carson even advocates "work projects" to provide incentive-based income to the poor while maintaining and beautifying the nation's infrastructure.[37]

The "New Jim Crow"

The economic imbalance between Blacks and Whites represents only one of the inequities of racialization. There also exists an enormous disproportion in the incarceration rates of Blacks and Whites. Michelle Alexander indicts the American criminal justice system that "imprisons a greater percentage of its Black population than South Africa did at the height of Apartheid."[38] Alexander says that African Americans

---

[33] Jackson, Jr., *The Truth in Black & White*, 189.
[34] Jackson, Jr., 189.
[35] Carson, *America the Beautiful*, 91.
[36] Carson, 176.
[37] Carson, 176.
[38] Alexander, *The New Jim Crow*, 6.

have been imprisoned on drug charges at rates twenty to fifty times greater than white men. "In major cities wracked by the drug war, as many as eighty percent of young African American men now have criminal records and are thus subject to legalized discrimination for the rest of their lives. These young men are part of a growing undercaste, permanently locked up and locked out of mainstream society."[39] Alexander attributes the absence of husbands and fathers in the black community to this phenomenon.

The startling reality behind these statistics reveals that they bear no correlation to crime ratios. In other words, the reason more Blacks are in prison than Whites (proportionately), is *not* because they commit more crimes. In fact, Alexander notes that Whites are more likely to engage in drug crime than people of color.[40] The difference in incarceration ratios has multiple causes, one of which is the coercive plea-bargaining tactics of prosecutors. Here's how it works: In an effort to get a conviction, a prosecutor will offer the suspect a reduced charge and lesser sentence if he agrees to plead "guilty," convincing him he will get the maximum sentence if he pleads "not guilty." Even if he believes himself to be innocent, the suspect is intimidated into taking the bargain, and he goes to prison. Another reason more Blacks are incarcerated is that Whites are more often able to afford a lawyer who knows the prosecutorial tactics and can get their clients off the hook.

Here's another almost unbelievable disparity: Until recently, the penalty for crack cocaine possession was far more severe than for powder cocaine. Most Blacks who use cocaine prefer crack to powder, possibly because it's cheaper. Alexandra Bonneau observes that the "sentencing disparity between crack cocaine and powder cocaine"

---

[39] Alexander, 7.
[40] Alexander, 7.

involved a "100-to-1 ratio."[41] Marc Mauer, Executive Director of the Sentencing Project, observes, "Defendants convicted of possessing as little as five grams of crack—the weight of two pennies—[received] a mandatory five years in prison."[42] According to Michael McNeil, "By the mid-1990s, it became apparent that African-Americans were subjected to a disproportionate number of federal crack convictions, along with their drastically heightened penalties. Meanwhile, those being convicted for possession of drugs without heightened penalties, such as powdered cocaine, were disproportionately white."[43]

This crack-to-powder sentencing disparity ultimately resulted in a "public outcry [that] demanded a decrease in the penalty associated with crack cocaine."[44] In 2007, the United States Sentencing Commission (USSC) passed USSG Amendment 706, an interim measure correcting the 100:1 crack-to-powder sentencing disparity, but the measure failed to eliminate mandatory minimum sentences.[45] However, according to McNeil, the amendment spurred Congress to address the issue. In August of 2010, with rare bi-partisan support, Congress passed the Fair Sentencing Act, which reduced the crack-to-powder sentencing ratio from 100:1 to 18:1, and eliminated mandatory sentencing guidelines for persons convicted of simple possession of more than 5 grams of crack.[46] Mauer called the vote "historic" and the

---

[41] Alexandra B. Bonneau, "Offensive Drug Offenses: Applying Procedural Justice Theory to Drug Sentencing in the United States and United Kingdom," *Boston University Law Review* 93, no. 4 (July 2013): 1486.

[42] Marc Mauer, "Beyond the Fair Sentencing Act," *The Nation*, December 27, 2010, 12.

[43] Michael McNeil, "Crack, Congress, and the Normalization of Federal Sentencing: Why 12,040 Federal Inmates Believe That Their Sentences Should Be Reduced, and Why They and Others Like Them May Be Right," *Mercer Law Review* 63, no. 4 (Summer 2012): 1360–61.

[44] McNeil, 1360-61.

[45] McNeil, "Crack, Congress, and the Normalization of Federal Sentencing," 1378.

[46] McNeil, 1379.

new law "a watershed event in the long campaign for a more rational approach to drug policy."[47]

These facts suggest that much of the persistent racial inequity in America has been due to systemic or structural causes, and the failure of white Christians to address these injustices widens the racial divide. Emerson and Smith's research into racialization and white insensitivity has left them deeply pessimistic about the potential for positive change. In fact, they describe their book as a "rather dismal portrait" of the prospects for improved race relations in the United States, and they lay much of the blame at the feet of Evangelicals.[48]

However, Emerson and Smith fail to acknowledge the sizeable contribution of Evangelicals to the reconciliation movement. Neither do they factor in the activity of God to affect change in race relations. Since the publication of their book in 2000, significant changes have occurred, especially in large Evangelical churches. The percentage of Evangelical mega-churches that are multi-ethnic has risen from 6 percent in 1998 to 25 percent in 2007.[49] David Campbell, a political scientist at Notre Dame, says, "If tens of millions of Americans start sharing faith across racial boundaries, it could be one of the final steps transcending race as our great divider."[50] Emerson has noted this more recent phenomenon and concedes that such rapid change "blows my mind."[51] Today many Evangelicals (as well as non-Evangelicals) engage in reconciliation efforts generating positive results.

Easing the Burden

Instead of ignoring or diminishing the awful realities of our history, Whites must own up to them. Instead of denying the truth of

---

[47] Mauer, "Beyond the Fair Sentencing Act," 12.

[48] Emerson and Smith, *Divided by Faith*, location 3501.

[49] David Van Biema, "Can Megachurches Bridge the Racial Divide?," *Time Magazine (Online Edition)*, January 11, 2010, 2.

[50] Van Biema, 2.

[51] Van Biema, 2.

racialization, we must encourage all reasonable efforts to change it.[52] Instead of blaming our black brothers for having a chip on their shoulder over the past, we should admit that it's more than a "chip." It's the crushing burden of centuries of injustice only recently made a little lighter, but still too heavy not to notice its unrelenting weight.

Let me close this chapter with a heartening story of how one group of white Evangelicals attempted to shoulder some of that burden.

"A Spiritual Earthquake"

In Jasper County, Texas, a group of white pastors invited black pastors in the area to a concert. After serving them a meal and treating them to an hour of musical entertainment, the white pastors stood together facing their black counterparts. Speaking on behalf of the white pastors, one of their number began to confess the sins of racism and injustice they and their forefathers had committed against the black community. Concluding his remarks, the speaker said, "Even though we don't deserve your forgiveness, we come before you and we ask you to forgive us." At that moment, as if on cue, the white pastors dropped to their knees. M.L. Johnson, an African American pastor who was present, described the moment as "a spiritual earthquake of immeasurable magnitude:"

> After about a 35 second period of silent shock, sadness, sorrow, and surprise, the sanctuary exploded under the pressure of relief from the need for repentance and forgiveness! The black audience, many silently weeping and visibly shaken, began to rise from their pews and move to the front where their white hosts were kneeling. Then they began to reach out and embrace their white brothers and sisters.[53]

---

[52] Many are discussing the possibility of reparations as a way to balance the scales of justice. For my treatment on this topic, see Chapter Eight.

[53] Melvin L Johnson, *Overcoming Racism... through the Gospel* (Longwood, FL: Xulon Press, 2007), 370-72.

Identificational Repentance and Forgiveness

This was a powerful demonstration of something called "identificational repentance," the idea that "individuals can repent by standing in the gap as a representative for the sins of others."[54] And this is a biblical idea. Daniel, Ezra, and Nehemiah identified with and repented for their fathers' sins. Reciprocally, Blacks should freely forgive. Some argue that the living have no right to forgive on behalf of the dead. Archbishop Tutu tells the story of Simon Wiesenthal, a Jew who refused to forgive a Nazi soldier's deathbed confession. Wiesenthal believed it would be presumptuous of him to do so, that it would trivialize the suffering of others. Tutu makes a compelling response to Wiesenthal. He tells of black South Africans who freely forgave on behalf of their dead and, in the process, found healing and closure for the pain of the past: "True forgiveness deals with the past, all of the past, to make the future possible. We cannot go on nursing grudges even vicariously for those who cannot speak for themselves any longer. We have to accept that [our act of forgiving is] for generations past, present, and yet to come. That is what makes a community a community."[55]

Interracial Small Group Gatherings

In order for members of multi-ethnic churches to experience genuine *koinonia* across racial lines, their pastors can provide settings where members can gather in small groups for learning, dialogue, repentance, and forgiveness. In such settings, after teaching on the relevant topics, pastors should explain the importance of identificational repentance, citing biblical, historical, and contemporary examples. Then, they can allow time in the meetings for members to express repentance and forgiveness among themselves. Chapter eleven of this book describes the "Journey to *Koinonia*," a small-group experience our church used for this very purpose. And my book by that title (*Journey to Koinonia*)

---

[54] Dawson, *Healing America's Wounds*, 93.
[55] Tutu, *No Future without Forgiveness*, 279.

gives a step-by-step "how-to" along with a facilitator's guide for those who want to lead a Journey in their church or group.

~~~~~~~~~~~

In our exploration of the chasm between the races, we have considered cultural differences, historical baggage, and the current challenges of corporate pain, racial insensitivity, and racialization. Now we turn to what might be the most challenging difference of all, the gaping political polarization of Blacks and Whites. Reconciliation advocate Alice Patterson calls politics "the Grand Canyon of Racial Division," and it is the subject of the next chapter.

7

POLITICS:
THE "GRAND CANYON of DIVISION"

"We can bring up race, pray together, forgive each other, and quickly agree to work toward our broader vision. ... However, the atmosphere changes when we add politics to the mix—especially Democrat vs. Republican. Things get tense. ...We're standing on the brink of the Grand Canyon of all divisions."
Alice Patterson

A grand old maxim says: "In essentials, unity. In non-essentials, liberty. In all things, charity." Applied to the current discussion, that means that *koinonia* does not depend on our seeing eye to eye on everything. Christian unity does not require uniformity. On the other hand, *koinonia* will not be achieved by ignoring our differences or pretending they don't matter. No, *koinonia* happens when we build a bridge to each other across those differences, and from that bridge, enjoy the scenic beauty of those varying landscapes.

We have seen the beauty of diversity—that ethnicity is a God-intended feature in the human family. We have also learned a little about our cultural differences—the ways we think, speak, and behave. On this bridge to *koinonia*, we have viewed our different histories. We acknowledged that for centuries Whites in America were the privileged, dominant class, and Blacks were the under-privileged and mistreated minority—especially in the South.

In this chapter, we're going to look at another major issue that, unfortunately, divides many Americans—even Christian Americans:

our political alignments. This issue is potentially the most volatile topic we will consider on our journey to *koinonia*. Alice Patterson, an author and advocate for racial reconciliation says,

> "We can bring up race, pray together, forgive each other, and quickly agree to work toward our broader vision. … However, the atmosphere changes when we add politics to the mix—especially Democrat vs. Republican. Things get tense. …We're standing on the brink of the Grand Canyon of all divisions. It is the deepest and widest breach. It's a gap between Black Christians who are mostly Democrats and White Christians who are mostly Republicans.[1]

Our differing political views are a result of our different histories, life experiences, and cultural lenses, especially the "identity lens" (see chapter four).

Black Republicans

Although the majority of black Christians tend to support Democratic candidates, it was not always that way. In the decades following the Civil War, most African Americans affiliated with the Republican Party.[2] After all, the Democratic Party had been pro-slavery prior to the War, and after the War, Democrats established Jim Crow laws in the South. For generations, they also opposed most of the civil rights legislation that would eventually pass in the 1960s.[3]

On the other hand, the Republican Party, founded by abolitionists, was the party of Lincoln and the Emancipation Proclamation. Every state Republican Party in the South was founded by Blacks. Frederick Douglass, former slave, outspoken abolitionist, and adviser to Lincoln, "eagerly attended the founding meeting of the Republican Party in

---

[1] Alice Patterson, *Bridging the Racial and Political Divide: How Godly Politics Can Transform a Nation* (San Jose, CA: Transformational Publications, 2010), 23.

[2] Barry D. Friedman, "Southern Politics: A Brief Explanation," *University of North Georgia*, 1, accessed February 23, 2014, http://faculty.ung.edu/bfriedman/Studies/sopol.htm.

[3] Alveda C. King, "A Covenant with Life," *The Black Republican*, Fall 2008, 17.

1854 and campaigned for its nominees."[4] The first directly-elected African American member of Congress was a Republican.[5] Republicans passed the Civil Rights Acts of 1866 and 1875, granting certain rights to Blacks and prohibiting discrimination against them in public accommodations. Republicans sponsored the thirteenth, fourteenth, and fifteenth amendments to the federal constitution, which, according to Lewis Gould, "were building blocks on which racial justice could later rest."[6] In his history of the Republican Party, Gould cites a comment by Frederick Douglass that the "Republican Party is the ship and all else is the sea," a view that would prevail among Blacks for six decades.[7]

Political Migration of Blacks to the Democratic Party

Defections from the Republican Party by African Americans occurred as early as 1908, when W.E.B. Du Bois endorsed William Jennings Bryan, the Democratic candidate for president, and urged Blacks to abandon their support for the Republican Party.[8] However, the migration of Blacks to Democratic ranks began in earnest during the presidency of Franklin D. Roosevelt, out of gratitude for his public works programs that provided jobs and eased Great Depression woes.[9] Nevertheless, most Blacks remained loyal to the Republican Party until the 1960s. Even Martin Luther King, Sr., affectionately known as "Daddy King," was a registered Republican.[10]

---

[4] *Black Republican History*, Article (National Black Republican Association, n.d.), http://www.nbra.info/index.cfm?fuseaction=pages.blackgop&.

[5] *About the South Carolina Republican Party*, Article (The South Carolina Republican Party), accessed February 23, 2014, http://www.scgop.com/about/scgop/. Joseph Rainey was elected in 1870 to represent South Carolina in the U.S. House of Representatives.

[6] Gould, *Grand Old Party*, Kindle e–book, 77.

[7] Gould, Kindle e–book, 67.

[8] Du Bois, *The Souls of Black Folk*, 202.

[9] Star Parker, *Uncle Sam's Plantation: How Big Government Enslaves America's Poor and What We Can Do about It* (Nashville, TN: Wind Books, 2003), 61.

[10] King, "A Covenant with Life," 17.

According to David Garrow, the major political realignment of Blacks can be traced to the 1960 presidential campaign. Martin Luther King, Jr. had been arrested for leading non-violent protests and was languishing in jail. Candidate John F. Kennedy personally telephoned Coretta Scott King to offer his help regarding her husband's incarceration. When Daddy King learned of this, he was so overcome with gratitude, that he publicly endorsed Kennedy for president. Many Blacks followed his lead.[11]

Black support for the Democratic Party continued to grow during the 1960s, for two reasons: First, the strong support of President Johnson for landmark civil and voting rights legislation, and second, the Republican Party's sudden shift toward more conservative policies such as Goldwater's states' rights emphasis.[12] Later, Nixon and Reagan continued to emphasize states' rights and "law-and-order" as key points of their platforms. While this appealed to conservative Whites, it alienated Blacks who viewed these issues as "racially-tinged."[13]

Another factor that pulled Blacks toward liberal politics was the failure of conservative politicians and white Christians to identify with the civil rights movement, especially in the South. In 1963, Dr. King wrote his famous "Letter from Birmingham Jail," in which he eloquently and passionately appealed to white pastors in the South to join the movement. King used biblical principles and Christian values as the basis of his appeal. Tragically, his words fell on deaf ears. Into that vacuum of support stepped northern liberal politicians and ministers who endorsed and marched with Dr. King, some of them giving their lives for the cause.

---

[11] Garrow, *Bearing the Cross*, 148.

[12] David A. Bositis, *Blacks and the 2012 Democratic National Convention* (Washington, DC: Joint Center for Political and Economic Studies, September 2012), 2, http://www.jointcenter.org/sites/default/files/upload/research/files/Blacks%20and%20the%202012%20Democratic%20National%20Conventio n.pdf.

[13] Cone and Wilmore, *Black Theology*, 5, 6.

But, more than all these, the event that sealed black support for the Democratic Party was the nomination of Barack Obama as the Democratic candidate for president. By 2008, 84 percent of African Americans identified with the Democratic Party.[14] Today, Blacks are the most loyal voting block of the Democratic Party.

Political Migration of Whites to the Republican Party

Just as black Christians were not always Democrats, white Evangelicals were not always Republicans. Their migration began during the 1960 presidential contest, when many Evangelicals supported Nixon as a reaction to Kennedy's Catholicism. They felt further pushed to the Right by the civil unrest and moral decline of the 1960s and 1970s. The assassination of JFK disheartened the younger generation, and as a result, many of them rejected authority structures and traditional values. The resultant "hippie movement" with its so-called "free love," student sit-ins, and take-overs of college campuses were seen as "liberal" causes that repulsed many morally-minded Christians, and frankly, scared them. James Cone and Gayraud Wilmore cite Nixon's "Southern strategy of law and order," as a factor that attracted many Whites who felt apprehensive of the increasing civil unrest and the new black militancy of the 1960s and 1970s.[15]

Add to all of that a series of decisions toward the secularization of America by an activist Supreme Court. These began with the removal of prayer and Bible reading from public schools in 1962 and 1963, followed by the 1973 Roe v. Wade decision that legalized abortion-on-demand. White Evangelicals saw a full-fledged culture war being waged by liberal politicians, and they fled to the Republican Party because of its socially conservative platform.

---

[14] David A. Bositis
[15] David A. Bositis

The Election of Barack Obama

The 2008 election of Barack Obama as the first black President of the United States was an epic event in American history. Furthermore, in 2012, Obama became the first Democrat since FDR to win the popular vote in back-to-back elections, and the first northern Democrat since FDR to be re-elected president.[16] Curtiss Paul deYoung, a white advocate for African Americans, calls Obama's election a *"kairos* moment:"[17] "What was proclaimed as a dream in August 1963 by Martin Luther King, Jr. is taking on flesh in the vision and ideals of Barack Obama. The dream is now physically manifested in reality. What was once seen as impossible is now visible. We are at the beginning of a remarkable new set of possibilities."[18]

Apparently, most African Americans agreed. Ninety-six percent of them voted for Obama in 2008, up from ninety-one percent who usually vote Democratic in national elections.[19] Among that ninety-six percent were the majority of black Pentecostals, whose support Obama secured by promising to stand firmly for traditional marriage. Interestingly, without the support of black Pentecostals, Obama could not have won the election.[20]

Many white conservatives opposed Obama, not because of his race, but because of concerns about his policies and social agenda, most notably his support for abortion-on-demand and later, his support for

---

[16] David A. Bositis, *Blacks and the 2012 Elections: A Preliminary Analysis* (Washington, DC: Joint Center for Political and Economic Studies, December 2012), 1–2, http://www.jointcenter.org/research/blacks-and-the-2012-elections-a-preliminary-analysis.

[17] Curtiss Paul DeYoung, *Coming Together in the 21st Century: The Bible's Message in an Age of Diversity* (Valley Forge, PA: Judson Press, 2009), Kindle e–book, location 1558.

[18] DeYoung., location 30.

[19] Patterson, *Bridging the Racial and Political Divide*, 125.

[20] Gaston Espinosa, "'Righteousness and Justice': Barack Obama, Pentecostals, and the 2008 Election," in *New Voices, New Visions: Future and Hope of Pentecostal Theology* (presented at the Society for Pentecostal Studies, Minneapolis, MN, 2010), 1.

same-sex marriage. Conservatives also worried about his campaign promise of "fundamental transformation" for America. Seeing in this a veiled plan to introduce socialist policies into the government, conservatives feared that such policies could reduce America to third-world status. They viewed Obama's liberal use of executive orders as circumventing the law of the land, and even dictatorial. Some expressed fears that Obama might stage a constitutional crisis by refusing to leave office after his second term. In retrospect, those fears seem laughable. But at the time, they were very real to those who harbored them.

On the other hand, many of Obama's supporters interpreted the constant criticism of the first African American president as rooted in racism. The point is, the political and racial tension in America was profound during the Obama administration.

The Election of Donald Trump

Talk about a political pendulum swing! To many, Donald Trump was as far to the right as Barack Obama was to the left. At the very least, the name "Trump" evoked strong reactions, in one direction or the other. Few people seem to be neutral in their perceptions of the 45th President of the United States. Those who support him, do so with passion. Those who oppose him, with equal passion, perhaps even with hatred. Alas, the stage is set once again for division, and that division is tinged with color.

A majority of black people, including black Christians, have serious concerns about Trump's record on race. For example, in 1973 and again in 1978 the Department of Justice sued his company for discriminating against potential black renters of his apartments. Then, in 2011, in a series of highly publicized TV interviews, Trump questioned Obama's eligibility for the presidency, suggesting that "he was not born here."[21] This charge forced Obama to reveal his long-

---

[21] Jemar Tisby, *The Color of Compromise*, 186.

form birth certificate to the public, and it left a cloud of perceived racism over Trump for questioning the legitimacy of the nation's first African American president. In 2015, Trump's call for a wall on the Mexican border was alleged by many to be inherently racist. For these reasons, some African Americans' attitude toward Trump could be characterized, not so much as hatred, but rather as fear. And they fear, not so much the man, but what they perceive as a white supremacy fervor in some of his most ardent followers. They fear a return to the violent thuggery and lynchings of the days of Jim Crow. Whether or not there is substance to these concerns, the fear is nevertheless very real.

African American Christians also question Trump's moral character, and they wonder how white Evangelicals, known for their support of family values, can vote for a man with multiple marriages and multiple allegations of extra-marital affairs. Because of those character flaws, many white Christians refused to vote for Trump, choosing a third party candidate or simply refusing to vote. The director of the Southern Baptist Convention's Ethics and Religious Liberty Commission called evangelical support of Trump "illogical." He also suggested that it hindered efforts toward racial reconciliation.[22]

Nevertheless, a Pew Research poll indicates that 81 percent of white Evangelicals voted for Trump.[23] Many of these did so because of his pro-life stance and because they opposed Hillary Clinton. They saw Trump as "the lesser of two evils." In fact, just before the 2016 election, one conservative Christian said to me, "The choice is between Nebuchadnezzar and Jezebel, and I seem to recall that Nebuchadnezzar did finally get saved." Which introduces another factor in white evangelical support for Trump. Some believe it is possible that he is a changed man. In fact, some see clear evidence of that change in his choice of Mike Pence as his VP.

---

[22] Tisby, 188.
[23] Tisby, 187.

Again, the point is, white Evangelicals and black Christians are still poles apart politically. This polarization didn't begin with Obama and Trump, but their elections certainly exposed it to a greater extent than ever before. And there is little evidence of that changing in the near future—especially in the South.

The South—Vortex of Political Polarization

According to David Bositis, "Culturally and demographically, the Republican Party has evolved since the 1960s from being a Midwestern and Northeastern party to being a Southern and non-coastal Western party. This evolution has profoundly affected the relationship between African Americans and the GOP."[24] In a research brief for the Joint Center for Political and Economic Studies, Bositis refers to "the racially polarized voting that defines much of southern politics."[25] Bositis attributes this polarization to the fact that the majority of the African American population in the country lives in the South, a region that has lately transitioned to "white conservative Republican political dominance."

These facts suggest huge challenges for black and white Christians in the South who are politically engaged, because political views frequently involve deeply-held convictions with strong emotional overtones. For example, white conservatives don't understand how black Christians can vote for a party with abortion and same-sex marriage as cornerstones of its platform. White Christians can get pretty worked up emotionally over that. After all, the Bible is clear in its disapproval of these practices. Consequently, they view black allegiance to the Democratic Party as a sell-out of biblical values.

---

[24] Bositis, *Blacks and the 2012 Democratic Convention*, 2.

[25] David A. Bositis, *Resegregation in Southern Politics?*, Reserach Brief, Civic Engagement and Governance Institute (Washington, DC: Joint Center for Political and Economic Studies, November 2011), 1, http://www.jointcenter.org/research/resegregation-in-southern-politics.

Remarkably, black Christians poll more conservatively on moral issues than white Evangelicals, so they are in full agreement with conservatives on issues like abortion and same-sex marriage. However, they wonder why these issues seem to take center stage at election time, yet stay on the back burner otherwise. A black friend of mine recently asked, "Why is it that Republicans have held the White House, along with majorities in the House and Senate and Supreme Court, yet they haven't passed legislation to address these moral issues? Is it possible they use these issues to garner votes at election time, yet have no intention of actually doing anything about them?" Meanwhile, black Christians find disheartening the utter silence of their white counterparts on the economic disparities that still plague American society, as discussed in the previous chapter. To them, it feels like one more hypocritical double standard.

Personal Reflections

My own story illustrates the tension politics can inject into an interracial church, and thankfully, the power of *koinonia* to diffuse that tension. At the time of the 2008 election, I was vexed over the fact that some of my black brothers and sisters intended to vote for Obama, including members of the church I pastored. I couldn't reconcile how they as Christians could support a man who stood for abortion rights. I felt so strongly about the matter that it threatened our relationship. Two things happened that totally changed my attitude.

First, through what I believe was a divine intervention, the Lord opened my eyes to see what I could never have seen on my own. It happened during a time of private prayer in which I had poured my heart out to God about my feelings. Over and over, I had pleaded, "Father, how can they do it? How can they know You and love You, yet support a man who stands for such an abomination?" I'm not sure how long I prayed, but after a while I grew quiet, and I sensed His gentle voice speaking to my heart. As thoughts poured from my spirit into my conscious mind, I began to write them down. The following is what I wrote:

"Imagine that you are part of a minority in a country that for centuries has been run by the dominant race. Your people have occupied the lowest class, lived in sub-standard housing, worked menial jobs, and barely had enough to get by. Everywhere you go, people size you up in an instant by one thing: the color of your skin. They stereotype you as dumb, lazy, immoral, dishonest, or just second class. Even though not one word has been exchanged, and they know nothing about you, they think they know it all. You feel their contempt.

"True, in the last 50 years there have been some amazing changes. You can eat in their restaurants, use their bathrooms, sit at the front of their buses. You can even live next door to them. Some of your race have broken through the glass ceiling and are getting opportunities at education and jobs, even professional jobs and political offices. Government programs like Affirmative Action have helped to level the playing field.

"Still, ancient prejudices run deep and die slowly. They run deeper than government programs can reach. Even though you now enjoy rights and privileges your forbears only dreamed of, many of the dominant race still manifest attitudes toward you that hark back to the old days. You still feel their contempt. And, in all honesty, you have developed some prejudices of your own. You find yourself stereotyping people on the basis of *their* race. You assume this person feels the same contempt so many of their kind have shown you for so long. And you have your defense mechanisms for handling that. The truth is, you feel there will never be a real leveling of the playing field.

"One political party seems to have championed the plight of minorities. They seem to offer programs that have meant the world to your social and economic improvement. Naturally, you support them with your vote. True, in recent years, that party has also supported issues you disagree with, and you're troubled by that. But how can you walk away from the Party that has stood by your people?

"Now a political candidate of your race rises like a meteor to national prominence. Never before has anyone of your race been nominated for president by a major party. In the past, those who sought the nomination were never taken seriously by mainstream movers and shakers. This time it's different. This man could actually be elected.

And what would it do for your people to have someone of your kind, with your background, who understands your plight, in the highest office in the land—the leader of the free world—the most powerful man in the world!

"How can you not support him?"

I knelt in that place of prayer for a long time, contemplating what I had "heard" and reading what I had written, again and again. This experience opened a window for me into the inner world of my black brothers and sisters, as if I were seeing the matter through their eyes.

Curiously, it didn't affect my vote in the election. Nor did it diminish my concern over the great moral issues of the day. I still longed for my black brothers and sisters to see these issues through my eyes. Nevertheless, this experience helped me see things through their eyes. It helped me understand why they voted as they did. It also gave me a newfound respect for them as committed Christians whose love for the Lord is just as strong and loyal as mine.

(Let me say again, one of the goals of interracial *koinonia* is simply to understand each other, not to convert each other to our political persuasion. Remember, *Koinonia* doesn't depend on uniformity. It doesn't require that we settle all differences. It calls us to accept one another *as we are* and let God sort out the rest.)

One other thing happened that put the black vote into perspective for me. It happened because of the *koinonia* I shared with a black elder in our church. He and I prayed together every week. In a conversation about the presidential election, he shared his heart on the matter. And because of the experience I just recounted, I was able to hear him. He explained the constant burden he carried over a generation of young black people who feel that, because of their race, they have no future. To their minds, the system is rigged against them, so they can never rise out of the poverty trap. He said, "An entire generation of our people is at risk, because they are convinced that nothing they do will matter, so why try?" This elder then said he felt that Obama's election could possibly spark hope for this young black generation, that seeing Obama break through the ceiling could inspire them to believe they also have a future. And, for that reason, he would vote for Obama. The tone of his explanation was almost apologetic.

Like my friend and elder, many black Christians find themselves conflicted when their moral values collide with matters of social justice. According to Robert Jones and Dan Cox, "African Americans strongly oppose same-sex marriage and some other hot-button cultural issues, … [yet, when it comes to their vote, they] rank these issues far below issues relating to the economy—job opportunities, minimum wage, education, and health-care."[26] They view these latter issues as every bit as biblical and moral as the former.

Which, again, points to the political divide that separates white Evangelicals and black Christians. Even though we agree strongly on the great moral issues, when it comes time to vote, we move in opposite directions. The Pew Research Center puts it this way: "It is an interesting feature of American politics that black Protestants and white Evangelicals share many views on social issues … yet they starkly diverge on their voting patterns. … Blacks focus more on civil rights and economic issues … than they do on the hot-button cultural issues that drive a large number of the white Evangelicals."[27]

"Learn to Listen"

So we come to the crux of the matter: White Christians zealously champion issues of moral righteousness, and therefore they support the political party that stands for those issues. Black Christians, because

---

[26] Robert P. Jones and Dan Cox, "African Americans and the Progressive Movement: A Background Report for Strategic Communications" (Center for American Values in Public Life, April 2006), 10.

[27] Scott Keeter and Luis Lugo, *Election 2004: Religion and Politics* (Pew Forum on Religion and Public Life, August 25, 2004), 3.

of their long and bitter familiarity with injustice, support the party that stands for social justice. Debates and arguments aimed at changing these political alignments are virtually pointless. They either fall on deaf ears or they arouse emotional defenses, leaving people more entrenched in their positions than before. Even carefully reasoned presentations supported with "facts" will not bring us together on these matters. In short, this is an unwinnable argument. And that is why we must not try to pound each other into political agreement. And above all, we must not postpone *koinonia* until we reach agreement.

On the other hand, candid dialogue on these issues, especially guided dialogue (see Chapter Eleven) can lead to authentic *koinonia*. By dialogue, I'm not referring to mere discussion. According to Peter Senge, "Dialogue differs from the more common 'discussion,' which has its roots with 'percussion' and 'concussion,' literally, a heaving of ideas back and forth in a winner-takes-all competition."[28] True learning begins with dialogue, which is "the capacity … to suspend assumptions and enter into a genuine 'thinking together.' "[29] Curtiss Paul DeYoung says, "As we dialogue with people from different cultural perspectives, we will need to 'learn to listen to voices and melodies that are unfamiliar to us.' These voices may hold the keys to … our desired unity."[30] Note DeYoung's words, "learn to listen." Listening to each other is the critical component in authentic dialogue, and it leads to biblical *koinonia*. Solomon said it like this: "The way of a fool seems right to him, but a wise man *listens*" (Prov. 12:15).

Meanwhile, we can dream, can't we?

One other thing. Let's not discount God's role in this matter. He could intervene into our political stalemate and do a totally new work in all

---

[28] Senge, *The Fifth Discipline*, 10.
[29] Senge, 10.
[30] Curtis Paul DeYoung, *Coming Together in the 21ˢᵗ Century: The Bible's Message in an Age of Diversity,* 166.

of us who love Him and bear His name. He could move us to "marry" moral righteousness and social justice, to join together to champion *both* ! We can certainly dream—and pray—for that to become reality. As we shall see in the next chapter, from a biblical perspective, moral righteousness and social justice are already "married." In fact, they form one inseparable, indivisible bond with each other. And both are essential facets of what the Bible calls "the way of the Lord."

8

THE ETHICS OF THE NEW COMMUNITY:
Righteousness and Justice

"For I have chosen him, in order that he may command his children
and his household after him to keep
the way of the LORD by doing righteousness and justice;
in order that the LORD may bring upon Abraham
what He has spoken about him."
Genesis 18:19

There are two words that every Christian believer ought to be thoroughly familiar with, because they are Bible words: Righteousness and Justice. Not only are they Bible words, but when used together, they create a catalytic combination that expresses one new amazing idea.[1] They also define what God calls "the way of the Lord."

"The Way of the LORD"

Would it be okay if I throw a couple of Hebrew words at you? Here goes: *Tsedaqah* (pronounced "sed-ah-kah") is the Hebrew word for "righteousness." *Mishpat* (pronounced "mish-pot") is the Hebrew word for "justice." (You will notice in the paragraphs that follow, that commentators spell these words in a variety of ways.)

---

[1] Graham Cray, "A Theology of the Kingdom," in *Mission as Transformation: A Theology of the Whole Gospel*, ed. Samuel Vinay and Chris Sugden (Eugene, OR: Wipf & Stock Publishers, 1999), 34.

In the Old Testament, these two words are often used together as a single figure of speech. In fact, very early in the Bible, God uses this figure of speech to describe what He calls "the way of the Lord." The occasion is the impending judgment on Sodom, and it involves one of several commissioning statements to His servant Abraham:

> And the LORD said, "Shall I hide from Abraham what I am about to do, since Abraham will surely become a great and mighty nation, and in him all the nations of the earth will be blessed? For I have chosen him, in order that he may command his children and his household after him *to keep the way of the LORD by doing righteousness and justice*; in order that the LORD may bring upon Abraham what He has spoken about him." (Gen 18:17-19 NASB)

As God tells Abraham what He is about to do to Sodom, He repeats words He first spoke to Abraham when He called him out of Ur of the Chaldees (Gen. 12:1-3). But, in this instance, He adds something new, namely, that one important way Abraham will bless all the nations of the earth is by teaching his children "to keep the way of the LORD by doing righteousness and justice." To get a handle on what that really means, let's contrast Abraham's value system with the extreme opposite of that—the outrageous immorality and injustice of Sodom.

Sodom: A Graphic Picture of Injustice

On the eve of Sodom's destruction, God informs Abraham that the "outcry of Sodom and Gomorrah is indeed great and their sin is exceedingly grave," and that He "will go down now and see if they have done entirely according to its outcry which has come to me" (Gen. 18:20, 21). Ready for another Hebrew word? "Outcry" (*ze aqa*) is a technical term for "the cry of pain or the cry of help from those who are being violated."[2] It was the word used when the Israelites cried out under their Egyptian taskmasters. It was also the scream of a woman being raped (Deut. 22:24, 27). The use of *ze aqa* in Genesis 18

---

[2] Wright, *The Mission of God*, 359. Wright's material is the source of this entire discussion on the linkage between God's judgment on Sodom and the commission of Abraham to do justice and righteousness.

leads to the inescapable conclusion that the sin of Sodom involved more than consensual homosexuality. It involved the aggravated sexual oppression of unwilling and vulnerable victims. Apparently, the people in the vicinity of Sodom suffered so intensely that their outcry against Sodom's injustice reached Heaven.

In the account of the angels' visit to Lot, we learn that "hostile, perverted and violent sexual immorality ... characterized 'all the men from every part of the city of Sodom—both young and old' (Gen. 19:4)."[3] The prophet Ezekiel adds another factor in his catalogue of Sodom's abominations: "Now this was the sin of your sister Sodom: She and her daughters were arrogant, overfed and unconcerned; they did not help the poor and needy. They were haughty and did detestable things before me" (Ezek. 16:49-50). Paraphrasing this passage, Christopher J.H. Wright describes the people of Sodom as "overproud, overfed, and underconcerned—a very modern sounding list of accusations."[4]

The scene of incomprehensible wickedness, including violent, perverted sexuality, greedy consumerism, and flagrant disregard for the needy, Sodom serves as the universal example of humanity at its worst. The way of Sodom is the extreme opposite of the "way of the Lord," and Sodom's fate forever stands as a reminder of God's righteous judgment on all such wickedness.

Abraham and the New Community: A Vivid Contrast to Sodom

For Sodom's sins, God would do the righteous thing: He would render justice to the oppressed by liberating them from their oppressors through a devastating judgment. In contrast to the people of Sodom, Abraham would "command his children and his household after him to keep the way of the Lord by doing righteousness and justice" (Gen. 18:19 NASB). These two ideas, God's intervention on behalf of

---

[3] Wright, 359.
[4] Wright, 360.

Sodom's victims and the values Abraham would model for his descendants, suggest the meaning of the terms "righteousness and justice." Are you willing to drill a little deeper into these two Hebrew words? The following calls for your "thinking cap," but I think you'll find it worth the effort.

Justice

In the Old Testament, the word "justice" (*mishpat*) can refer to decisions, matters of jurisprudence, legal rights, and commandments of the *Torah*, among others.[5] The word also commonly involves defending and delivering victims of oppression and aiding the vulnerable (especially widows, orphans, the poor, and ethnic minorities),[6] as in the following verses:

- "The LORD works righteousness and *justice* for all the oppressed" (Ps. 103:6).

- "Learn to do good; seek *justice*, reprove the ruthless; defend the orphan, plead for the widow" (Isa. 1:17, NASB).

- "For if you truly amend your ways and your deeds, if you truly practice *justice* between a man and his neighbor, if you do not oppress the alien, the orphan, or the widow, and do not shed innocent blood in this place, nor walk after other gods to your own ruin, then I will let you dwell in this place, in the land that I gave to your fathers forever and ever" (Jer. 7:5-7, NASB).

Many such passages could be cited to demonstrate that justice, in the sense of defending and aiding the vulnerable, is a common Old Testament theme.

Righteousness

The word "righteousness" (*tsedaqah*) also enjoys a variety of uses, and is sometimes interchangeable with *mishpat*. Theologian Bo Johnson

---

[5] Bo Johnson, *"Mispat,"* in *Theological Dictionary of the Old Testament*, ed. G. Johannes Botterweck, Helmer Ringgren, and Heinz-Josef Fabry, trans. David E. Green, vol. 9 (Grand Rapids, MI: Eerdmans, 1998), 89–95.
[6] Johnson, 91.

notes the similarity between the two words, yet makes an important distinction:

> The two terms *sedeq* and *mispat* are often used parallel and seem synonymous.... Such parallel usage, however can also indicate intensification. When God's *mispatim* come, the inhabitants of the world learn *sedeq* (Isa. 26:9). The king is to judge his own people with *sedeq* and his poor with *mispat* (Ps. 72:2).... Yahweh... loves *sedaqa* and *mispat* (Ps. 33:5).... The two terms *mispat* and *sdq,* however, are not synonymous. The semantic field of "decision, judgment, law" attaches to *mispat,* while *sdq* focuses on the principle of "what is right, correct."[7]

Johnson's concept of righteousness as "what is right, correct" suggests the idea of measuring up to a standard, such as God's standard of moral and ethical purity as expressed in the *Torah.*

Often, *tsedaqah* is used as a verb in the sense of acquitting or vindicating a person, declaring them right. This usage suggests the Apostle Paul's concept of righteousness as an active, declarative work of God on behalf of the believer, best expressed in the word *justify* (Rom. 3:26). Isaiah uses the word in a similar way: "The One who *justifies* me is near; who will contend with me?" (Isa. 50:8, HCSB). In this verse, the Messiah rests in hope that God will vindicate Him, declare Him righteous. In a subsequent passage, the Messiah bears the sin of others and justifies many: "As a result of the anguish of His soul, He will see it and be satisfied; by His knowledge the Righteous One, my servant, will *justify* the many, as He will bear their iniquities" (Isa. 53:11 NASB). One remarkable Old Testament passage contains multiple uses of *tsedaqah,* along with *mishpat:* "Do not deny justice (*mishpat*) to your poor people in their lawsuits. Have nothing to do with a false charge and do not put an innocent or honest (*tsedaqah*) person to death, for I will not acquit (*tsedaqah*) the guilty" (Exod. 23:6-7).

---

[7] Bo Johnson, "*Sadaq,*" in *Theological Dictionary of the Old Testament,* ed. G. Johannes Botterweck, Helmer Ringgren, and Heinz-Josef Fabry, trans. Douglas W. Stott, vol. 12 (Grand Rapids, MI: Eerdmans, 2003), 247–48.

As Hebrew terms, both *tsedaqah* and *mishpat* are concrete and active, something people are to *do*, not just ideas people contemplate. To define them in the simplest possible terms, righteousness means to do what is right, morally and ethically; justice means to put right what is wrong or neglected.[8]

A Catalytic Combination

A catalytic reaction occurs when *tsedaqah* and *mishpat* are joined together. They form an indivisible bond that makes the two concepts inseparable. In other words, you can't have one without the other. Wright says, "They form what is technically called a 'hendiadys'—that is, a single complex idea expressed through the use of two words."[9] A good way to define the combined words might be the English couplet: "moral righteousness and social justice."

Vertical and Horizontal

Moral righteousness involves a vertical accountability to God for foundational spiritual and moral issues such as exclusive worship of the LORD, the sanctity of human life, and the sanctity of marriage. These issues are "foundational" because the Creator established them at the dawn of creation and later codified them in the Ten Commandments. Moral righteousness involves fidelity to God as both Creator and Lord over creation. God's command "be holy" (Lev. 19:2) issues from His own holy nature and involves a catalogue of moral and ethical requirements (Lev. 19:2-37). Those requirements include exclusive worship of the LORD (vv. 4, 5-8), keeping the Sabbath and respecting parents (v. 3), sexual morality (vv. 20-22, 29), rejection of idolatry and the occult (vv. 26-31), and personal integrity (vv. 35-36).

Social justice, on the other hand, has to do with horizontal relationships between fellow human beings. In His monologue in

---

[8] I am indebted to my friend Ed Nelson for suggesting this definition.
[9] Wright, *The Mission of God*, 366–67.

Genesis 18:17-19, the LORD expresses confidence that Abraham would "command his children and his household after him *to keep the way of the* LORD by doing righteousness and justice." Moses would later define the "way of the LORD," leaving no doubt as to its meaning: "For the LORD your God ... shows no partiality and accepts no bribes. He defends the cause of the fatherless and the widow, and loves the alien, giving him food and clothing. And you are to love those who are aliens, for you yourselves were aliens in Egypt" (Deut. 10:17-19). In describing the LORD's "ways," which He "made known to Moses," the psalmist says, "The LORD works righteousness and justice for all the oppressed" (Ps. 103:6-7). The ethical requirements in Leviticus 19 that define holiness also include social responsibilities such as providing for the poor, (vv. 9-10), economic justice to employees (v. 13), consideration for the disabled (v. 14), protection for ethnic minorities (vv. 33-34), and judicial integrity (vv. 12, 15).

Social justice is not only addressed in the *Torah* and Psalms. It is also a common theme in the prophets (Amos 5:21-24, Micah 6:8), the teachings of Jesus (Luke 4:18-19), and the Epistles (Gal. 2:10). Clearly, Scripture calls the people of God to care for the disadvantaged. The sheer preponderance of verses on the subject makes it impossible to read the Bible without seeing them. Yet many in the Church have managed to overlook them. Pastor Rick Warren once confessed with admirable candor, "I've got three advanced degrees. I went to two different seminaries and a Bible school. How did I miss the 2000 verses in the Bible where it talks about the poor?"[10]

What About Reparations?

Applied to the present discussion, this raises the issue of reparations, a subject that evokes varying and even volatile responses. Nevertheless, any serious contemplation of justice must include a conversation about restitution for past injustices. To begin with, because of the massive devastation caused by centuries of slavery and

---

[10] Carl Cannon, "Man on a Mission," *Reader's Digest*, March 2009, 162.

racism, any consideration of reparations will involve a role for the federal government. And the idea is not without precedent. After World War II, the American government gave $20,000 to each Japanese-American it had confined to internment camps, along with an official apology.[11]

Incredibly, freed slaves did not receive such consideration after the Civil War! A century later, when Martin Luther King, Jr. lobbied the American government for a public works program that would guarantee jobs and a minimum wage to poor Blacks, his appeal fell on deaf ears!

Jamar Tisby, an African American author, concedes that the idea of government-funded reparations "raises all kinds of questions about practicality, such as how to determine which black people are actually descendants of slaves and who counts as black in a socially constructed paradigm. These and other concerns present valid obstacles to the implementation of reparations, but they should not stop the conversation altogether."[12]

Like Tisby, I don't know the answers to those questions, but I believe the time for the conversation has come. Perhaps the following observations can help to inform that conversation.

In June of 2012, I attended the Summer Institute at the Duke Divinity School Center for Reconciliation, an international symposium on race relations. One of the presenters was Pumla Godobo-Madikizela, author of *A Human Being Died That Night: A South African Story of Forgiveness*. Pumla is a South African who lived under the Apartheid regime for many years, and then served on the Truth and Reconciliation Commission formed by the Nelson Mandela government. The Commission was the black South Africans' response

---

[11] Jemar Tisby, *The Color of Compromise,* 199.
[12] Tisby, 197.

to their white oppressors. As its name implies, the Commission focused on reconciliation rather than retaliation. The guilty were required to face their victims or victims' families and confess their crimes, after which they were forgiven. In cases warranting punishment, it was meted out humanely and even mercifully. The work of the Commission helped prevent horrible reprisals that might otherwise have shaken the nation and tainted the new government.

In my interview with Pumla, I specifically asked for her views about reparations. Her response was instructive: "Reparation comes from the word 'repair.' As an indicator of his desire to fully repair the relationship, the perpetrator offers reparation."[13] She cited the biblical example of Jacob's reunion with Esau. Approaching Esau, Jacob sent gifts ahead of him as a way of acknowledging his sin and his willingness to make it right.

Curitss Paul DeYoung agrees, adding that reconciliation remains incomplete without reparations: "Costly reconciliation calls us not only to forgive but to repair wrongs committed, whether or not we were the offending party."[14]

The concept of reparations is consistent with biblical restitution. Speaking of this, Tisby says, "Saying 'I'm sorry' is not enough. Expressing remorse may begin the process of healing, but somehow that which was damaged must be restored. The [Old Testament] law goes on to state that the wrongdoer 'must make full restitution for the wrong they have done, add a fifth of the value to it and give it all to the person they have wronged (Num. 5:7)."[15] Zacchaeus went beyond that requirement when he received Christ and repented of his

---

[13] Pumla Gobodo-Madikizela, interview by Terry Roberts at Duke Divinity School, May 29, 2012.

[14] Curtiss Paul DeYoung, *Reconciliation: Our Greatest Challenge—Our Only Hope* (Valley Forge, PA: Judson Press, 1997), 103.

[15] Jemar Tisby, *The Color of Compromise*, 200.

wrongdoing. He promised to repay those he had cheated *fourfold* (Luke 19:8).

Chris Rice and Spencer Perkins believe Affirmative Action has been an attempt, though meager, at restitution. However, they question its survivability, because it forces one group to make sacrifices for another group without providing the heart motivation necessary for such sacrifices. They add, "Christianity is a voluntary enterprise. Looking to the interests of someone else works best when it is a choice one makes."[16]

That observation does not dismiss the need for some kind of federally-funded restitution for Blacks, but it does suggest a role for other entities besides the government. Glenda Wildschut agrees: "All sectors of society have a role to play in contributing to reparations. Large corporations and individual citizens could do a great deal to indicate their willingness to contribute to making up for the wrongs of the past. Similarly, the churches and other faith-based institutions can play an important part in facilitating healing processes."[17]

Since the church is the arena where I serve, I can speak with some knowledge about the healing potential it can bring to this issue. Although no single church can repair the massive damage of the past, every church can do something to relieve the present suffering of people who live under the fallout of those sins. For example, Tisby encourages white churches to declare a "literal or figurative 'year of Jubilee' for black people. They could pool resources to fund a massive debt forgiveness plan for black families. … These monies could fund educational opportunities or down payments on houses. … Wealthier churches could fund a salary for a [bi-vocational] black pastor to work

---

[16] Perkins and Rice, *More than Equals*, location 1973.
[17] Glenda Wildschut, "Human Rights: The South African Experience," in *The Wiley-Blackwell Companion to Religion and Social Justice*, ed. Michael D. Palmer and Stanley M. Burgess (Malden, MA: Wiley-Blackwell, 2012), 517.

full time in the church and exponentially increase the minister's capacity to serve in the local community."[18]

When churches engage in compassionate outreach to hurting people, it speaks volumes about their concern for "the least of these," and wins the heart of the community. When churches do not, it makes them irrelevant in the eyes of the community. Harry Jackson and Tony Perkins suggest that "some of the anti-Christian rhetoric in the public square is a result of the world *hearing* us more than *seeing* us. And if the church is not visibly seen serving the poor of our communities, we will become irrelevant to the next generation."[19]

Jackson and Perkins cite churches that serve the poor, not only through emergency food relief, but also through educational and employment services, computer labs, help with home ownership, and savings programs.[20] Churches can also serve the needs of working single mothers by providing after school programs for their children, something our church has been doing for several years.

On this topic, Usry and Keener raise these sobering questions: "Will U.S. Christians sacrifice their own luxuries to provide college scholarships for children from single-parent homes who otherwise could not afford it? Or will we let them remain part of the permanent underclass to which their educational status and economic background will normally consign them?"[21]

The white church can and must demonstrate that reconciliation is more than a kind word or gesture. It also involves compassionate action.

---

[18] Jemar Tisby, *The Color of Compromise*, 200.
[19] Harry R. Jackson, Jr. and Tony Perkins, *Personal Faith, Public Policy* (Lake Mary, FL: FrontLine, 2008), 113–14.
[20] Jackson and Perkins, 113–15.
[21] Usry and Keener, *Black Man's Religion*, location 1789.

Here's a suggestion: If you decide to host a "Journey to *Koinonia*" in your church or group (see Chapter eleven of this book), consider bringing this topic in to a dialogue session in Meeting 5 ("Present Challenges"). Rather than just throwing the general topic of reparations wide open to opinions, ask the participants to dialogue about specific steps the local congregation can take to help repair the sins of the past. The pastor could present the ideas suggested in the previous paragraphs as examples. Also, encourage dialogue about the systemic causes of injustice along with practical solutions. Members should pray, brainstorm, and then implement initiatives to address tangible needs in their community, as a living demonstration of repentance. Such initiatives could furnish the seed bed for transformative relationships between Whites and Blacks.

The Cross Metaphor

Given the vertical and horizontal relationships implicit in *tsedaqah* and *mishpat,* the catalytic combination of the two words suggests that moral righteousness and social justice are inseparable. One cannot exist without the other. "Righteousness and justice form one quality, not two. The Old Testament knows no division between social justice and private morality."[22]

Just as the cross contains two planes, the vertical and the horizontal, and cannot exist without both, so any consideration of the Church's ethics must include both moral righteousness and social justice. Jesus' citation of the Great Commandment established this: "'Love the Lord your God with all your heart and with all your soul and with all your mind.' This is the first and greatest commandment. And the second is like it: 'Love your neighbor as yourself.' All the Law and the Prophets hang on these two commandments" (Matt. 22:37-40). The Apostle John implies the same with his question: "He who does not love his

---

[22] Cray, 34.

brother whom he has seen, how can he love God whom he has not seen?" (1 John 4:20 NKJV).

This carries enormous implications for the American Church, which suffers from a lamentable and potentially tragic polarity. Christians have championed these terms as separate concepts and drawn up battle lines to defend them in the current culture war. White Evangelicals most often rally to moral righteousness causes, such as the sanctity of life and marriage; yet they have the regrettable history of having passively dismissed or even openly resisted the civil rights movement. Black and Hispanic Christians, on the other hand, tolerate immoral planks in the Democratic Party platform, because the Party champions the cause of social justice.

Here's the bottom line truth of the matter: There can be no ultimate social justice without moral righteousness. Those who would pull the moral underpinnings from this nation in an effort to achieve social justice will end up with neither. Without a sense of ultimate accountability to God and His moral law, justice becomes whatever those in power determine it to be. Under such a system, when the oppressed do manage to achieve power, they often become the new oppressors, continuing the cycle of injustice. The infamous gulags of Soviet Communism are a case in point. Absolute moral standards are essential to inform social justice. Just as the horizontal beam of the cross hangs on the vertical, in the same way, social justice depends on moral righteousness. On the other hand, a "moral righteousness" that does not lead to social justice is a mere waxwork.

The Church must come together and insist on both, refusing to follow any cause that favors one to the neglect of the other. In simple terms, this means white Evangelicals must repent for their absence from the civil rights movement and their complicity in ongoing systemic injustice. They must also withhold support from the Republican Party whenever it elevates politics above principles. For their part, black Christians must reconsider their unswerving loyalty to the Democratic Party—a party that has repeatedly desecrated the biblical and moral convictions of black Christians.[23]

Happily, significant influencers in the Church are calling for such a coming together. A number of years ago, I attended a press conference in the nation's capital where white and black leaders gathered to address the racial and political division within the Church. African American pastor Harry R. Jackson was among those leaders, and I was moved by his stirring words: "It is time for those in the Church who stand for moral righteousness and those who stand for social justice to come together. And when they do, there will be an explosion of the glory of God in this nation, and the Church will become an

---

[23] Some Black leaders are doing this. The Coalition of African American Pastors (CAAP), representing more than 4,000 black pastors, pulled their support from Obama's re-election effort. (C-SPAN broadcast, National Press Club, July 31, 2012, Washington, D.C., http://www.c-span.org/Events/Black-Clergy-Group-Opposes-Pres-Obama-on-Gay-Marriage/10737432751/ (accessed September 3, 2012).

unstoppable force for good."[24] Jackson's words suggest the catalytic power of righteousness and justice that could result in a national revival.

Whether that happens or not, one thing is certain: God will fulfill His mission to bless the nations of the earth "by the existence in the world of a community that will be taught to live according to the way of the LORD in righteousness and justice."[25] Those words, "the way of the LORD in righteousness and justice," define the ethics of the New Community. They also inform its culture, which is Christ-centered and Spirit-empowered *koinonia*, the subject of the next chapter.

---

[24] This press conference was called by the Family Research Council in conjunction with a two-day event called "The Pastors' Briefing." Jackson's words here are a paraphrase of his comments based on my personal recall.

[25] Wright, *The Mission of God*, 369.

Part 3
Experiencing *Koinonia*

We have seen God's eternal purpose for the Church—that it showcases to powers and principalities that Jesus Christ can remove the barriers that divide human beings and unite in one Body people from every nation, ethnicity, and culture. We have explored our differences: the cultural, historical, and political distinctives that make us who we are. We have learned that *koinonia* does not require us to deny these differences, but to seek to understand them. Now, it's time to move forward into an authentic relationship with each other that submits our differences to Christ, and leaves them with Him. That's the whole point of this book.

In this section, I will also share some practical steps that can help a local church or group experience biblical *koinonia*. That happened in our church through a six-week, interracial small group experience we call "**Journey to *Koinonia***," and I'm going to explain it in Chapter Eleven.

First, I want to explore the true nature of *koinonia*—what it is and how it works—from a biblical perspective. Then, let's look at the New Testament admonition to "accept one another" just as we are, with all our differences, faults, and disagreements, and pursue fellowship with each other.

It's time to experience *koinonia* !

9

THE CULTURE OF THE NEW COMMUNITY:
Christ-centered and Spirit-empowered *Koinonia*

If righteousness and justice are the ethics of the Church, *koinonia* is its culture—it's way of life. The implication of this is that, while we pursue justice, we must also pursue *koinonia*. We must not wait until our differences are settled and all injustices corrected before we come together. God calls us to pursue fellowship with each other in the midst of our faults and disagreements.

In order to pursue *koinonia*, we would do well to know more about it. What does it look like? How does it behave? As previously stated, one component of *koinonia* is table fellowship, but it involves much more than that, as we shall see in this chapter.

The King James Version translates *koinonia* as "fellowship" (Acts 2:42), "communion" (2 Cor. 13:14), and "contribution" (Rom. 15:26). The NIV also renders it as "partnership" (Phil. 1:5) and even "generosity" (2 Cor. 9:13). Obviously, no single English word captures the richness of this concept. In secular Greek usage, the word applied to business partnerships and other close relationships including marriage.[1] Applied to the Church, *koinonia* has been defined as "the symbiotic relationship of the believer with other believers."[2]

---

[1] Friedrich Hauck, "Κοινωνία," in *Theological Dictionary of the New Testament*, ed. Gerhard Kittel, trans. Geoffrey W. Bromiley, vol. 3 (Grand Rapids, MI: Eerdmans, 1965), 798.

[2] James T. Flynn, Wie L. Tjiong, and Russell W. West, *A Well-Furnished Heart: Restoring the Spirit's Place in the Leadership Classroom* (Fairfax, VA: Xulon Press, 2002), 153.

An Extension of Old Testament Community

New Testament *koinonia* is an "extension of the Old Testament concept of community that existed from the creation of mankind, was developed in the people of Israel, and expanded upon in Jesus Christ and His Church."[3] The Hebrew word for that Old Testament concept of community is *khaver*, which can mean "associate," "friend," "partner," "colleague," or "esteemed fellow-student."[4] The verb form of the word, *khavar*, can mean to "join," "befriend," "assist," and "fasten" (as in securing or binding one thing to another).[5] Hence, the Hebraic concept of community involved a strong, unbreakable bond, a sense of corporate identity. Hellinger says, "Judaism places great emphasis on the strong bond between the individual and the community; that is, on the crucial role of the community in the life of the individual. Traditionally and by the very terms of Jewish discourse, being part of the Jewish collective means belonging to the Jewish people as well as to the Jewish religion."[6] Indeed, the worst calamity a Hebrew could contemplate was separation from his community, as evident in the *Torah's* penalty for serious offenses: "Whoever commits any of these detestable sins will be cut off from the community of Israel." (Lev. 18:29 NLT).

Sharing with Christ

The believer's first and primary *koinonia* is with Jesus himself. As Hauck notes, "According to 1 Corinthians 1:9, Christians are called to fellowship with the Son. ... They are lifted up to be his fellows. They enter into a spiritual communion with the risen Lord."[7] For Hauck, the Lord's Supper provides the optimum setting for experiencing this fellowship with Jesus. He considers the bread and wine "vehicles of

---

[3] James T. Flynn, Wie L. Tjiong, and Russell W. West, 135.

[4] Marcus Jastrow, *"Chavar,"* *A Dictionary of the Targumim, the Talmud Babli and Yerushalmi, and the Midrashic Literature* (New York, NY: The Judaica Press, 1971), 421.

[5] Jastrow, 421.

[6] Hellinger, "Judaism: Historical Setting," Kindle e-book, 170.

[7] Hauck, "Κοινωνία," 804.

the presence of Christ" and those who partake, "Christ's companions."[8] "Thus the nature of the Lord's Supper is expounded by Paul in terms of fellowship with the person of Christ, namely [*koinonia*] with His body and blood (1 Cor 10:16)."[9] In saying this, Paul would have his reader know that the exalted Christ with whom he fellowships is none other than the historical Jesus who died to make such *koinonia* possible.[10]

Sharing with Other Believers

Because the Lord's Supper is a community activity, a coming together of believers around the bread and wine, it implies *koinonia* with one another through Christ. It also necessarily involves considerateness and liberal forgiveness toward other believers. Paul had this in mind when he cautioned believers about partaking "in an unworthy manner" (1 Cor. 11:27). One may infer from the context that unworthiness at the Lord's Table has more to do with horizontal relationships than with vertical, as Paul's final word on the matter suggests: "So then, my brothers, when you come together to eat, wait for each other … so that when you meet together it may not result in judgment" (1 Cor. 11:33-34).

Hauck notes that Christians also share other things in common besides the person of Christ and His table. They share a new nature (2 Pet. 1:4). They have drunk of the same Spirit (1 Cor. 12:13). They make up one body and share the same hope (Eph. 4:4). They share the same precious faith and a common baptism (v. 5). They share the same "God and Father of all, who is over all and through all and in all" (5:6). Christians share in suffering persecution and the ensuing comfort provided by the Spirit (Phil. 1:7; 2 Cor. 1:5-7).[11]

---

[8] Hauck, 805.
[9] Hauck, 805.
[10] Hauck, 805.
[11] Hauck, 804–6.

Sharing Material Goods

Paul appeals to Gentile believers to share their material goods with their poorer Jewish counterparts (Rom. 15:27). Hauck observes, "Since Gentile Christians have acquired a share in the spiritual blessings of the original community [they] are thus under obligation to help the latter with material goods."[12] Several New Testament references containing the word *koinonia* use it in the context of voluntary financial assistance to other believers in their hardship (Rom. 15:26; 2 Cor. 8:4, 9:13; Heb. 13:16). Hence, sharing material goods among believers is essential to biblical *koinonia*.[13]

Near the end of the second century, the North African theologian Tertullian described this aspect of *koinonia* in the Christian gatherings of his time:

> If he likes, each puts in a small donation; but only if it he wants to and only if he is able. There is no compulsion; all is voluntary. These gifts are, as it were, piety's deposit fund. For they are not taken and spent on feasting and drinking-sessions, but to support and bury poor people, to supply the wants of needy boys and girls without parents, and of house-bound old people. . . . People say, See how they love one another. . . . One in mind and soul, we do not hesitate to share our earthly goods with one another. We have all things in common except our wives.[14]

Christine Pohl notes that such sharing of material resources helped early Christian communities rise above their social divisions: "In emphasizing that both provision and welcome came as grace, the early Christians shared their lives and possessions with one another and transcended significant social and ethnic differences."[15] In a similar vein, John Perkins comments that "the body of Christ must be marked

---

[12] Hauck, 807.

[13] Hauck, 796.

[14] Tertullian, *Apology*, trans. T.R. Glover (Cambridge, MA: Harvard University Press, 1966), 39.

[15] Christine D. Pohl, *Making Room: Recovering Hospitality as a Christian Tradition* (Grand Rapids, MI: Eerdmans, 1999), Kindle e–book, location 1200.

as an alternative social order that 'breaks the cycle of wealth and poverty.'"[16]

Sharing Table Fellowship

In chapter one, I underscored table fellowship as an essential component of *koinonia*. More on that here. According to Pohl, "Hospitality is a way of life fundamental to Christian identity."[17] One aspect of hospitality, the sharing of meals, expresses and strengthens *koinonia*. as Pohl relates:

> I learned to cherish potluck dinners where you were never entirely sure what you were eating but it usually tasted good, and the fellowship tasted a bit like the Kingdom. … [W]e were learning to welcome one another across racial and socioeconomic differences. With a profound commitment to racial reconciliation as an expression of the power of the gospel, we have pushed past the superficial layers of friendliness to the deeper strata of respect, care, and honesty.[18]

Ben Witherington and Darlene Hyatt describe table fellowship as an aspect of "shared living."[19]

Ethnic and cultural differences hindered table fellowship in the church at Rome, a situation that evoked strong admonitions from the Apostle Paul (Rom. 14:1-4). According to Witherington and Hyatt, Paul's concern over dietary issues

> stems from the compelling need to maintain table fellowship in the … Roman house-churches. … Shared meals prefigure, reveal, and reflect the Kingdom. … Eating was and still often remains a bounded activity, and so, when we intentionally include others in such times, social, economic, and cultural boundaries are transcended through the

---

[16] Charles Marsh and John M. Perkins, *Welcoming Justice: God's Movement toward Beloved Community* (Downers Grove, IL: InterVarsity Press, 2009), Kindle e–book, 29.

[17] Pohl, *Making Room*, Kindle e–book, location 22.

[18] Pohl, Kindle e–book, locations 24–30.

[19] Ben Witherington and Darlene Hyatt, *Paul's Letter to the Romans: A Socio-Rhetorical Commentary* (Grand Rapids, MI: Eerdmans, 2004), 348.

relationship forged at the common table. Such is the subversive aspect of hospitality.[20]

To understand the importance of table fellowship, one need only recall Paul's confrontation with Peter and Barnabas in Antioch when they stopped eating with their Gentile brothers and sisters (Gal. 2:11-21). *Koinonia* necessarily involves hospitality that brings people together around a common table. At its essence, then, *koinonia* is simply doing life together, not only with one's own kind, but also with believers different from oneself who love the same Lord.

Sharing Forgiveness

When Paul appealed to the close bond between Philemon and himself as a reason for showing mercy to the runaway slave Onesimus (Philem. 7), he had more in mind than mere friendship. He was reminding Philemon that they shared a common, precious faith in the same Master. They shared a corporate identity with the same community. They shared a *koinonia* that superseded every personal consideration. Burgess adds, "Here is the suggestion that their common faith superseded social conventions of the period. The result is that Philemon frees Onesimus—a clear signal to the rest of the early church that their new community in Christ should come before old practices."[21] The following statement describes this adhesive power of *koinonia:*

> At conversion, a new believer is baptized into the Body of Christ and becomes a part of the organic whole called the Church. The resulting fusion of a new believer's life to the Body of Christ, His Church, results in a kind of glue called fellowship or *koinonia* that hold the Body of Christ together as one.... The result is an organic living Body that represents Christ's love, nature, and authority to the world. This holy assembly of called out ones, bound together with the glue of fellowship, are Christ's witness to the world..... It is this sense of community that was the context for teaching, maturity, and growth in Christ. The bond

---

[20] Witherington and Hyatt, *Romans,* 346.
[21] Burgess, "Christianity: Historical Setting," Kindle e-book, 47.

of community also fused diverse peoples together across racial and cultural divides.[22]

The use of glue as a metaphor for *koinonia* is insightful and deserves elaboration.

The Adhesive Power of *Koinonia*

Some adhesives work because of a chemical reaction involving two or more ingredients. Similarly, biblical fellowship involves two essential elements believers share in common. The first is Christ Himself. Very different kinds of people find their unity in their mutual love for Jesus, which transcends all other distinctions. Paul alludes to this when he says of Jesus, "He himself is our peace" (Eph. 2:14). In other words, Jesus draws all believers to Himself, and in drawing us to Himself, He draws us to each other. In Him, though we are different, we are one. Archbishop Desmund Tutu puts it like this:

> There is a movement, not easily discernible, at the heart of things to reverse the awful centrifugal force of alienation … and disharmony. God has set in motion a centripetal process, a moving toward the center, toward unity … and justice, a process that removes barriers. Jesus says, "And when I am lifted up from the earth I shall draw everyone to myself" as he hangs from His cross with outflung arms, thrown out to clasp all … in a cosmic embrace, so that everyone … belongs. … All distinctions make for a rich diversity to be celebrated for the sake of the unity that underlies them. We are different so that we can know our need of one another, for no one is ultimately self-sufficient. … It was God's intention to bring all things in heaven and on earth to a unity in Christ, and each of us participates in this grand movement.[23]

The second component in the adhesive of *koinonia* is the presence and activity of the Holy Spirit, who actualizes the presence of the living Christ in the hearts and lives of believers. Paul says, "Both [Jews and Gentiles] have access to the Father by the one Spirit" (Eph. 2:18). The Holy Spirit intensifies the sense of Jesus' presence when two or more believers come together in His name (Matt. 18:20), and they experience

---

[22] Flynn, Tjong, and West, 135-36.
[23] Tutu, *No Future without Forgiveness*, 265.

"the unity of the Spirit" (Eph. 4:3). According to Gordon Fee, "The 'unity of the Spirit' does not refer to some sentimental or esoteric unity that believers should work toward. Rather, Paul is speaking of something that exists prior to the exhortation. ... Their lavish experience of the Spirit, which they have in common with all others who belong to Christ, has made them members of the one body of Christ."[24]

Reflecting on the spiritual fruit of Azusa, where the Holy Spirit united believers of many ethnicities and nationalities, Cecil M. Robeck, Jr. observes:

> [T]he Azusa Street Mission provides a glimpse of what is possible if we allow space for the Holy Spirit to change hearts and minds. It may also provide a model for congregations in our own day to embrace this same kind of diversity, to demonstrate before the world the power of the gospel to break down the artificial racial and ethnic walls that otherwise divide us.[25]

"A Bell and a Pomegranate"

The fruit of the Spirit may not be as sensational as the gifts, but they are just as needful, if not more so. The truth is, the fruit and the gifts are not mutually exclusive. On the contrary, they work best together, as the "love chapter" of the Bible makes clear.[26]

When God instructed Moses to design garments for the Old Testament high priest, He specified an intriguing ornamentation at the hem of the robe: "A bell and a pomegranate, a bell and a pomegranate, all around the hem of the robe to minister in."[27] This beautifully

---

[24] Gordon D. Fee, *God's Empowering Presence: The Holy Spirit in the Letters of Paul* (Peabody, MA: Hendrickson Publishers, 1994), 701.
[25] Cecil M. Robeck, Jr., *Azusa Street Mission and Revival: The Birth of the Global Pentecostal Movement* (Nashville, TN: Thomas Nelson, Inc., 2006) 14.
[26] 1 Corinthians 13
[27] Exodus 39:26

suggests the environment in which the Holy Spirit prefers to minister—where both the gifts and the fruit function together.

Paul, who gave us the list of nine "charismatic" gifts in 1 Corinthians 12, also gave us a list of nine fruit of the Spirit, the ingredients most essential to the "unity of the Spirit." Read Paul's well-known words in light of interracial relationships:

> But the fruit of the Spirit is love, joy, peace, longsuffering, kindness, goodness, faithfulness, gentleness, self-control. Against such there is no law. And those who are Christ's have crucified the flesh with its passions and desires. If we live in the Spirit, let us also walk in the Spirit. Let us not become conceited, provoking one another, envying one another.[28]

This unity of the Spirit functions without the need for temporal "compatibility," to use a term from Henri Nouwen's imaginative description of *koinonia*, which he sees as

> the grateful recognition of God's call to share life together and the joyful offering of a hospitable space where the recreating power of God's Spirit can become manifest. Thus all forms of life together can become ways to reveal to each other the real presence of God in our midst. Community has little to do with mutual compatibility. Similarities in educational background, psychological make-up, or social status can bring us together, but they can never be the basis for community. Community is grounded in God, who calls us together, and not in the attractiveness of people to each other. ... The mystery of community is precisely that it embraces *all* people, whatever their individual differences may be, and allows them to live together as brothers and sisters of Christ and sons and daughters of his heavenly Father.[29]

So, the defining elements in the culture of the New Community, love for Jesus and unity of the Spirit, create this extraordinary *koinonia*. No other community in the world understands such love. No other people experience a "unity of the Spirit" that can bridge every divide.

---

[28] Galatians 5:22-26

[29] Henri J. M. Nouwen, *Making All Things New: An Invitation to the Spiritual Life,* [Large print ed.], (San Francisco, CA: HarperSanFrancisco, 1981), 82-83.

However wonderful, *koinonia* does not come without determined effort. Because of its centrality to the Church's life and mission, the Enemy fights it. The barriers of ethnicity, culture, and politics often hinder it. Therefore, believers must cultivate it intentionally. Understanding the challenges involved in this, Paul appealed to the Church in Asia Minor: "Be completely humble and gentle with each other; be patient, bearing with one another in love. *Make every effort* to keep the unity of the Spirit in the bond of peace" (Eph. 4:2-3).

When he wrote the church at Rome, Paul addressed this issue through the use of a Greek word, *proslambano*, a word we will study at length in the next chapter.

10

ACCEPT ONE ANOTHER:
Proslambano

As Paul sat in Rome under house arrest, writing to the Ephesian believers about the wonderful unity-within-diversity that characterizes the Church, perhaps his mind turned to words he had previously penned to the divided Roman church on the same topic. In the first part of his Epistle to the Romans (chapters 1-11), Paul established the theological foundation for a unified Church. In the second part (chapters 12-16), he explained how that works in practice. In fact, beginning in chapter 14, he devotes a rather lengthy passage on how two very different groups of people can find harmony.

When I wrote my doctoral dissertation, I did a thorough study of this passage. Would you bear with me and allow me to share that with you here? Prepare yourself. My writing style over the next few paragraphs is necessarily scholarly because of the nature of the document I was writing. Even though it may be a bit dense, I hope you'll wade through it, because I think you'll find this passage in Romans as fascinating as I did:

> Paul begins this section with the command, "Accept him whose faith is weak" (14:1), and concludes it with a similar one: "Accept one another" (15:7). Gordon Fee suggests, "This repeated imperative … serves as a kind of inclusio."[1] (In biblical studies, an inclusio is a literary device that brackets off a section of text by using the same word at the beginning and end of the section.) Paul not only uses the word "accept" at the beginning

---

[1] Gordon Fee, *God's Empowering Presence*, 617.

and end of this passage, he uses it twice more within the passage. He argues that God has accepted others who are different from us (14:3) and that "Christ accepted you" (15:7).

The Greek word translated "accept" (*proslambanō*) comes from a root word (*lambano*) meaning "to take," as in *taking* a wife. Jesus used it in His call to every would-be disciple to "*take* his cross and follow me" (Matt. 10:38).[2] So it involves an intentional embracing of someone or something so as to make them part of one's life. Burghard Siede says the compound form, *proslambanō* means to "take along" and carries a "theological importance when meaning 'admit into fellowship.' ... Paul exhorts the Romans to seek out those who have a weak faith, because strong and weak are equally accepted into fellowship with God through Christ's death."[3] Karl Donfried adds the illuminating comment that the command involving *proslambano* applies to one who is not already a close friend.[4] In other words, Paul wants believers to reach out to those beyond their existing circle of friendship, to people they might consider "strangers."

The mention of "strangers" brings to mind Paul's earlier imperative, "practice hospitality" (Rom. 12:13). The term *hospitality* is far more instructive in the Greek, where *philoxenia* literally means "love (*philos*) of strangers (*xenos*)." According to William Mounce, "*Xenos* functions as a noun to describe someone who is a foreigner or a stranger to a group in question."[5] Sociologists use *xenos* to create the technical term "xenophobia," meaning fear of other cultures.[6] On this note, Witherington argues, "Christians are called to be 'strangers in the world,' aware of our own essential 'otherness' so that fear of

[2] Burghard Siede, "Take, Receive," in *New International Dictionary of New Testament Theology*, ed. Colin Brown, vol. 3 (Grand Rapids, MI: Zondervan, 1978), 747–48.

[3] Siede, 751.

[4] Karl P Donfried, ed., *The Romans Debate* (Peabody, MA: Hendrickson Publishers, 1991), 110.

[5] William D. Mounce, "Strange(r)," *Mounce's Complete Expository Dictionary of Old and New Testament Words* (Grand Rapids, MI: Zondervan, 2006), 686.

[6] Lane, *A Beginner's Guide to Crossing Cultures*. Kindle ed., location 506.

strangers gives way to divinely enabled *philoxenia* ('love of strangers')."[7]

One wonders how Paul's language could be stronger or clearer. Just as Jesus called His disciples to inconvenience themselves for His sake by *taking* their cross, Paul calls the Roman Christians to go out of their way to *take* believers from the other side of the cultural divide into their fellowship. This will not require changing their personal convictions, but it will require laying aside any demands for uniformity. The obedience of faith to which Paul calls his audience is "an obedience which entails believing, loving, serving, uniting with other believers, however different their lifestyles may be."[8]

Paul has nothing less than this in mind when he urges Gentiles to "bear with the failings of the weak and not to please ourselves. Each of us should please our neighbor for his good, to build him up" (15:1-2). This exhortation follows his previous challenge to "pursue the things that make for peace and the building up of one another" (14:19, NASB). Speaking of this "peace" Fee says, "Such *shalom* among the people of God, empowered by the Spirit, results from their 'pursuing' it with diligence. It means at times giving up 'one's own good' for the sake of others."[9]

Here's the upshot of this passage from Romans: If we will listen to the voice of the Spirit within us, we will preserve the unity of the Spirit among us, as Paul exhorts in Ephesians 4:4. If we allow the Spirit to reproduce His love for others in us, we will find ourselves drawn to other people in whom He dwells—even people different from ourselves. In other words, the Spirit of God in me will help me identify with the Spirit of God in you (because He is the same Spirit) and will pull me toward you. As the Bible says, "Deep calls unto deep."[10]

---

[7] Witherington and Hyatt, *Romans*, 349.
[8] Witherington and Hyatt, 38.
[9] Fee, *God's Empowering Presence*, 621.
[10] Psalm 42:7 NKJV

To leave no doubt as to what it means to preserve the unity of the Spirit, Paul explains it in the clearest terms: "With all humility and gentleness, with patience, showing tolerance for one another in love."[11] Now, read those words again, and this time read them through the lens of interracial relations within the church.

In other words, Paul is saying that because we love Jesus, and because His Holy Spirit dwells within us, we can choose to subordinate every issue and every concern to His purpose for the Church. We can surrender our culture, our tradition, our history, our politics, even our own identity to Him. We want Him to have it all, because He is Lord of His Church, and therefore, He is Lord of me. I'm not saying that we give up our culture or tradition, only that we surrender them to His greater purpose.

"I surrendered my 'blackness' to Jesus"

A few years ago I attended a men's conference at which Bishop Larry Jackson was the featured speaker. Bishop Jackson is an African American church leader and Promise Keepers speaker. Commenting on 2 Corinthians 5:17 ("If anyone is in Christ, he is a new creation; old things have passed away; behold, all things have become new") and Galatians 3:28 ("There is neither Jew nor Greek, slave nor free, male nor female, for you are all one in Christ Jesus"), Jackson said, "When I became a new creation in Christ, I surrendered my 'blackness' to Jesus. Now, 'black' is not my dominant culture, Christ is. In turn, Christ sanctified my blackness and gave it back to me to use in service to Him. Now, I can enjoy my black culture and all that goes with it, but it no longer controls me. Christ does."

That statement, coming from a black man, inspired me to do the same with my "whiteness." To surrender it to Christ so it no longer controls me. To surrender it to Christ so that He can use it to serve others "with

---

[11] Ephesians 4:2 NASV

162

all humility, and gentleness, with patience, showing tolerance for one another in love."

In Ephesians, Paul says that God is carrying out a plan which He will accomplish through His Son, Christ Jesus. That plan is to display the beauty of Christ through a diverse yet united Church, showing forth God's wisdom—His majestic genius—to the principalities and powers in the spiritual realm. And God's plan is succeeding.

The Man on the Cross

Before closing this chapter, let me tell you a story that beautifully illustrates that point. In February of 1971, African American pastor John Perkins lay in a hospital recovering from years of stress as a civil rights leader in Jackson, Mississippi. The founder of an inner city ministry called Voice of Calvary, Perkins not only preached the gospel of salvation through Jesus Christ, but he also sought justice for poor Blacks all around him. For his efforts, he was severely persecuted by white authorities. A year earlier, policemen had arrested Perkins on trumped up charges, and they beat him nearly to death in the town jail.

Now sick, exhausted, and disillusioned, he began to question the validity of his lifelong labor for the cause of justice. Struggling with feelings of hatred toward his white tormentors, he seriously considered leaving the church and joining the black nationalists. Then, an image began to form in his mind, the image of Jesus hanging on the cross. As he considered this, it seemed he could hear Jesus saying, "Father, forgive these people, for they don't know what they're doing."[12] Perkins recalls the experience in these words:

> His enemies hated. But Jesus forgave. I couldn't get away from that. The Spirit of God kept working on me … until I could say with Jesus, "I forgive them, too." I promised Him that I would "return good for evil." … And He gave me the love I knew I

---

[12] John Perkins, "Reconciliation" (lecture presented at the Summer Institute, Duke University Center for Reconciliation, May 29, 2012).

would need to fulfill His command to ... "love your enemy." Because of Christ, God Himself met me and healed my heart and mind with His love.[13]

Perkins returned to his work with a renewed commitment, not only to seek justice, but also reconciliation across racial lines. He would go on to found the community development movement, also known as the faith-based movement, which has been recognized by presidents of the United States. "At its best, the community development movement seeks to reclaim, and to make more explicit, the theological commitments that animated the civil rights movement—'redemption, reconciliation and the creation of beloved community'—and to put these commitments to the test in building community among the poor and the excluded."[14]

A few years ago I heard John Perkins tell this story at The Summer Institute sponsored by the Duke University Center for Reconciliation. After John's message, I stood in line to meet him personally. As we shook hands, he took a genuine interest in me, asking about matters of mutual interest. Rarely have I been in the presence of a man who exuded the love of God as that man did, both in his public ministry and in private conversation.

John Perkins illustrates the divine priority for the people of God. He was so overwhelmed by the Love that flowed from the Man on the cross, it changed the course of his life. Instead of a crusader for hatred and violence, John became an ambassador of love and unity.

The love that flows from the Man on the cross has the power to unite mortal enemies. That love empowers us to love and forgive one another, knowing that God Himself has forgiven us and will ultimately

---

[13] John Perkins, *Let Justice Roll Down* (Ventura, CA: Regal, 2006), Kindle e-book, locations 1917–20.
[14] Marsh, *The Beloved Community*, location 144.

right every wrong. That is the real hope we can offer every victim of injustice.

As the people of God, we are called to be His agents for reconciliation in our divided society. That mission requires our commitment to the ethics of the New Community—righteousness and justice. We must also commit to the culture of the New Community—Christ-centered and Spirit-empowered *koinonia*. Interracial fellowship centered in Jesus and empowered by the Holy Spirit will serve as a potent adhesive holding believers together despite their differences, and it will display to a divided world the manifold (multi-colored) wisdom of God.

The next chapter suggests a practical and powerful way to help people experience *koinonia* across their differences.

Rev. John Perkins with the author
Duke Divinity School Center for Reconciliation
Summer Institute, 2012

11

JOURNEY TO *KOINONIA*:
A Small-group Experience

This chapter describes a six-week, small-group experience I conducted with fourteen members of Trinity Church, where I serve as Lead Pastor. Half of the participants were white and the other half were black. We called the experience "Journey to *Koinonia.*" For those who would like to conduct their own "Journey," I refer you to the companion to this book, *Journey to Koinonia: An Interracial Small Group Experience.* It contains more detailed information about the experience, along with step-by-step instructions, copies of materials used, and a Facilitator's Guide.

The weekly meetings on our Journey provided opportunities for the participants to: 1) hear teaching on a series of relevant topics; 2) share and listen to one another in guided dialogue sessions so as to better understand each other's life journey; 3) experience interracial *koinonia* through the spiritual and relational atmosphere of the meetings; 4) express repentance and forgiveness; and 5) become a model for future multi-ethnic small group experiences.

Preparation

Before the Journey could begin, a series of preparatory steps were necessary. These steps included recruiting participants, planning the meetings, writing the curriculum, and creating instruments to measure outcomes.

Selecting and Recruiting Participants

A few concerns guided the selection of participants: First, I wanted the group evenly divided along racial lines. Second, I sought variety in age and gender. I intentionally chose a few older people who could recall the days of Jim Crow. On the younger end of the spectrum, I wanted a certain measure of maturity—people with sufficient life experience to inform their contribution to the group and responsible enough to fulfill expectations.

Journey Participants by Race, Age, and Gender

Black	Age		White	Age
Female	31		Female	32
Female	32		Male	38
Male	56		Female	39
Female	57		Male	41
Female	63		Female	57
Male	64		Male	57
Female	71		Female	76

Due to the potential volatility of some of the topics, I looked for people with the capacity to demonstrate respect for others. I also chose participants at varying stages in their spiritual walk and in their understanding of race relations. Those who ultimately accepted my invitation included seven Blacks and seven Whites, for a total of fourteen participants. Including my wife and me, the group totaled sixteen. However, due to occasional absences, the six meetings averaged fourteen in attendance.

The participants represented a range of political ideologies. We administered an anonymous questionnaire with five political options, which yielded somewhat surprising results (see Table below).[1] Remarkably, two Blacks indicated they were "conservative," and the only "liberal" in the group was white. One black participant selected

---

[1] For copies of the pre-journey and post-journey questionnaires, see my book *Journey to Koinonia: An Interracial Small Group Experience*.

"other" and specified, "All the above, depending on the issue." I used the terms "liberal" and "conservative" on the questionnaire to ascertain whether participants tend to vote Democratic or Republican. However, in retrospect, the labels "conservative" and "liberal" appear inadequate and potentially misleading, because the same individual can hold liberal sentiments about certain issues and conservative leanings about others. Instead of using these labels, I suggest you simply ask the participants to identify which political party they usually vote for.

Table 1: Journey Participants by Political Ideology

Ideology	Black	White
Conservative	2	5
Liberal		1
Moderate		1
Prefer not to say	4	
Other(please specify)	1 ("All the above, depending on the issue.")	

Finally, the participants represented the following vocations: one educator, one retail manager, one graphic artist, one self-employed, one retired teacher, two government service employees, three clerical workers, and one homemaker. One participant receives disability retirement, and another is in the process of applying for disability.

Planning the Meetings and Pre-Session Reading

In order to maximize impact, the meetings would require a number of components. First, they should begin on a spiritual note, with a few minutes of worship and prayer. In order to honor the diverse musical tastes among the participants, I would ask them to take turns choosing and leading a song to open each meeting. This proved as simple as a sing-a-long using recorded music. Second, since each meeting revolves around a particular topic reflected in teaching and dialogue, I had to write the curriculum and prepare dialogue questions for the meetings.

(Happily for those interested in doing their own "Journey," that curriculum is now contained in this book!)

Because of the importance of honest dialogue, I devised rules of engagement to guide this process. These "rules" included a concept known as "talking to the campfire," which allows participants to share their thoughts in a non-threatening way.[2] I cannot overstate how important dialogue is in achieving interracial *koinonia*.

Third, a time of fellowship over food would provide informal interaction among the participants and potentially reduce the intensity of the encounter. I decided to ask participants to volunteer to bring the food.

As a location for the meetings, I chose a multi-purpose room in our church so we could arrange chairs as needed and set up refreshments. Concerning the day and time for the meetings, I decided to give the participants a say in that matter—something determined in the orientation meeting. Because several of the participants had small children, I arranged childcare for each of the meetings, with our church bearing the expense.

Curriculum and Dialogue Questions

My preparation for our first Journey involved writing the curriculum—the material we would teach in each session. Since then, I have gathered all of that material into one concise format—the book you are holding right now! So, I recommend this book as the primary textbook for your Journey experience. I would also recommend two other books to your participants as additional resources: *Let Justice Roll Down*, the autobiography of John Perkins, and *Bridging the Racial and Political Divide: How Godly Politics Can Transform a Nation* by Alice

---

[2] I borrowed this concept from Edgar H. Schein (*Organizational Culture and Leadership*, 391-92), and I explain it in more detail in my book *Journey to Koinonia: An Interracial Small Group Experience*.

Patterson. These two books approach the racial divide from entirely different yet equally legitimate perspectives. (I ordered these books online and gave them to our participants at the orientation meeting, our church bearing the expense.)

Power Point presentations were used for most of the teaching sessions. I also used several video clips for illustration purposes. The dialogue questions were carefully prepared ahead of time and designed to complement each week's teaching topic. I also set up a resource table at each meeting with dozens of books and videos related to the various topics we considered. I created a list of these resources, arranged by topic, for each participant.

Meeting Topics

In order for participants to bridge the divide of race, culture, history, and politics, they must understand these issues. Therefore, teaching was an important component of each meeting. As previously mentioned, the curriculum is now contained in this book, and includes six broad topics:

> **Orientation Session:** "God's New Community" (Chapter 2)
> **Meeting One:** "The Beauty of Diversity" (Chapter 3)
> **Meeting Two:** "Cultural Differences: Seeing Life through Different Lenses" (Chapter 4)
> **Meeting Three:** "Our Shared History: Walking on Sacred Ground" (Chapter 5)
> **Meeting Four:** "Politics: The Grand Canyon of Division" (Chapter 7) and "Righteousness and Justice: The Way of the Lord" (Chapter 8)
> **Meeting Five:** "Present Challenges: Racial Insensitivity, Racialization and Corporate Pain" (Chapter 6)
> **Meeting Six:** "The Culture of the New Community: Christ-centered and Spirit-empowered *Koinonia.*" (Chapter 9)

The Power of Dialogue

Before closing this chapter, let me say again how essential guided dialogue is to interracial relationships. It was a vital component in our weekly meetings and contributed greatly to the positive outcomes of the Journey. According to Curtiss. Paul DeYoung, honest dialogue accelerates interracial relationships and leads to *koinonia*.[3] Consider the following statements about dialogue:

"We believe that every person is created in the image of God and therefore has dignity, worth, and something of value to share. So we must develop the art of listening. This will be particularly challenging as we try to listen to those whose experience in life is very different from ours. As we dialogue with people from different cultural perspectives, we will need to 'learn how to listen to voices and melodies that are unfamiliar to us.' These voices may hold the keys to unlocking the doors that open our minds to the essential components for creating our desired unity."[4]

"Dialogue is the way of community. It is the personal dimension of sharing. Dialogue concretizes the will to be in relation with another person. It is the self-conscious response of an individual with another self. It is the form of the personal; it is the way of the willed encounter, a means of grace, a celebration of shared meaning. Dialogue is the way of explored intention, the way of God who is always seeking to share himself with others."[5]

"There are bound to be differences and disagreements when people dialogue. When everyone is given a voice, a greater number of outlooks are laid out on the table. These are the moments that reveal whether our respect for the other person is genuine. For unity to be maintained, we must sincerely believe that people can disagree and still love God. One of the most damaging things in the Christian community is the spirit of judgmentalism. This spirit creeps in when one professed believer doubts

---

[3] DeYoung, *Reconciliation*, 69.

[4] Curtiss Paul DeYoung, *Coming Together in the 21st Century: The Bible's Message in an Age of Diversity*, 166.

[5] James Earl Massey, *Spiritual Disciplines* (Grand Rapids: Zondervan, 1985), 71-87. Quoted in Curtiss Paul DeYoung, *Coming Together in the 21st Century: The Bible's Message in an Age of Diversity*, 225.

the faith of another professed believer because of a difference of opinion or belief on a particular issue."[6]

The Bible on Dialogue:

- "The way of a fool seems right to him, but a wise man listens ... A fool shows his annoyance at once, but a prudent man overlooks an insult. ... Reckless words pierce like a sword, but the tongue of the wise brings healing." Prov. 12:15-18
- "My dearly loved brothers, understand this: everyone must be quick to hear, slow to speak, and slow to anger, for man's anger does not accomplish God's righteousness." James 1:19-21
- "Let your conversation be gracious and attractive so that you will have the right response for everyone." Col. 4:6

With these verses in mind, Peter Senge's definition of dialogue takes on added meaning: "Dialogue differs from the more common 'discussion,' which has its roots with 'percussion' and 'concussion,' literally, a heaving of ideas back and forth in a winner-takes-all competition."[7] True learning begins with dialogue, which is "the capacity ... to suspend assumptions and enter into a genuine 'thinking together.'"[8] Reflecting on the benefit of cross-cultural dialogue, Michael Pocock and Joseph Henriques add:

> "When we take time to be with people, a relationship is developed. Both parties drop their masks; they respect each other's convictions and understand each other's sufferings. ... As we listen to our friend's real beliefs and problems, we divest our minds of the false images we may have harbored, and we are determined also to be real. ... We no longer

---

[6] Curtiss Paul DeYoung, *Coming Together in the 21st Century: The Bible's Message in an Age of Diversity,* 166).
[7] Senge, *The Fifth Discipline*, 10.
[8] Senge, 10.

173

desire to score points or win a victory. We love the person too much to boost our ego at his or her expense."[9]

On that note, Edgar Schein's concept of "talking to the campfire" proves especially helpful in interracial dialogue. This is a non-persuasive form of dialogue that avoids eye contact. Instead of looking directly at the other members of the group, the person sharing looks down at the "campfire" while speaking. Thus, the objective is not to persuade or convert others to their point of view but to open a window into their life experiences and resulting perspectives, along this line: "This is what I have experienced in life and that is why I see things as I do." Of course, since our meeting was held inside the church building, we didn't use a literal campfire. We set a candle on the floor in the middle of the group, and encouraged participants to look at it while speaking.

Because most of the participants had little or no previous relationship with each other, other than worshiping together on Sundays, I wanted to allow them time to develop a level of comfort with each other before launching into difficult themes. Therefore, I decided to advance the intensity of the dialogue slowly throughout the six-week Journey, beginning with milder topics in the early meetings and moving to more difficult subjects in later meetings. Remarkably, by the fourth meeting, the participants began asking if they could forego the "campfire" and talk to each other directly!

Results of the Journey
It would be virtually impossible to quantify the results of an experience like the "Journey to *Koinonia*." How do you count heartaches and healing hugs? How do you measure hidden fears and falling tears? Or the nuances of hope as it dawns in a heart? Only God can count those

---

[9] Michael Pocock and Joseph Henriques, *Cultural Change and Your Church: Helping Your Church Thrive in a Diverse Society* (Grand Rapids, MI: Baker Books, 2002), 158.

things. So, I decided to use a "qualitative" approach to evaluate the results of the Journey.

The evaluation involved two questionnaires, one administered prior to the Journey and the other afterwards. The pre-Journey Questionnaire contained eleven essay-type questions asking for the participants' experiences and perceptions about various racial, cultural, and political matters. The post-Journey Questionnaire contained seven questions asking participants to evaluate the Journey, share any change in perceptions they experienced because of it, and offer advice about replicating and improving the Journey. In addition to the questionnaires, I also considered verbal and written comments from participants and observations from the actual meetings.

At the time we implemented the Journey, three goals had been uppermost in my mind:

> First, that participants begin to experience *koinonia* across racial lines—something our multi-ethnic church needed in greater measure.

> Second, to foster a deeper level of understanding between the two cultures. I wanted participants to view a number of pertinent issues through each other's lenses and experience moments of insight that would enlighten and perhaps dispel previous assumptions. Thus, cross-cultural understanding was a secondary goal of the Journey.

> Third, because reconciliation is a prelude to *koinonia,* I wanted participants to experience and express repentance for personal sins and to identify with the sins of their forefathers. I hoped that victims of these sins would offer forgiveness, and that some would even experience inner healing as a result.

The evidence suggests that in varying degrees, several participants realized one or more of these goals. Here are a few comments from the evaluation:

- "Yes, I definitely feel that we of both cultures have a much better understanding and greater appreciation of each other. ... We will be less likely to misunderstand the positions of cultures different than ourselves."
- "The dialogue helped me better understand each person's life journey and what has brought them to their beliefs and convictions."
- "We had some really great conversations where I felt comfortable being honest about my viewpoints and they seemed comfortable doing the same."

In the final meeting, we separated the participants by gender and gave them an opportunity to express repentance and/or forgiveness, and (for those who desired) to wash each other's feet. In the women's session, an incident occurred that my wife later related to me in the following words:

> Ashley (a young white woman) spontaneously knelt in front of Lindsey (an older black woman) and began to sob. She shared that about two weeks into this Journey, she learned that her great grandfather had been in the KKK. She shared her shock and grief over learning that her family had inflicted pain on people of color. Ashley then asked Lindsey to forgive her and her family. Lindsey responded, "You couldn't help it, Ashley. You had nothing to do with it. But I forgive your family for what they did."

The following comments sent by email from another white participant, reflect a similar experience:

> I am broken over the fact that I never involved myself regarding race issues, as I just felt as long as it does not affect me, I do not want to get involved. I am not a confrontational person, but a peacemaker, therefore, just did not let racial issues become my concern. That has changed during this journey. I never realized the suffering, humiliation,

and rejection other non-white races suffered. I have experienced a truly broken heart now that my eyes are open to their suffering, so much so that after our meeting I went home, prayed and asked God to forgive me for my lack of concern.

Another white participant explained his empathy toward a black participant who tearfully described his "hurt and dismay" over racial discrimination: "You cannot help but feel compassion and sorrow for the wrongful actions by others."

For the a more complete account of the results of our Journey, along with the questionnaires and other materials, I refer you again to my book *Journey to Koinonia: An Interracial Small Group Experience.*

~~~~~~~~~~~~~~

Preparing this book for publication has required me to review the material you have just been reading. The emotional and spiritual experiences recorded in the accounts of the six meetings and the responses of the participants, have moved me deeply—again. In some measure, I have relived those wonderful meetings. This has whetted my appetite for more "Journey" experiences in the future. I hope it has also inspired you to go on your own "Journey to *Koinonia.*"

CONCLUSION

In contrast to the uniformity and exclusiveness that often characterize the present social order, God's "New Community" (the Church) expresses the divine delight in diversity; it embraces people of vastly different backgrounds who share a common devotion to Jesus; and, it experiences a fellowship that transcends every temporal distinction.

This community is on mission with Jesus to gather people from every nation and ethnicity into one body for the glory of God. That mission began with the call of Abraham and continues in the Great Commission Jesus gave to His Church. Central to that mission are the ethics of the New Community, righteousness and justice, a catalytic combination forming one powerful "weapon" against the prejudice and oppression of a broken world (2 Cor. 6:7).

Members of the New Community share a mutual love for Jesus and a common experience with the Holy Spirit. These two factors produce a bond that holds dissimilar members together, a bond expressed in the Greek word *koinonia* and suggested in Paul's phrase "the unity of the Spirit" (Eph. 4:3). *Koinonia* involves sharing everything from food to finances, and pared to its basic sense, means "doing life together."

Within a spiritual and relational small-group setting, honest dialogue can bring participants to understand and appreciate our differences and learn to accept one another as Christ has accepted us.

Bibliography
(Arranged by Category)

Biography

Collier, Trina. *Biography of Martin Luther King, Jr.* n.p.: Hyperlink, 2012. Kindle e-book.

Gifted Hands: The Ben Carson Story. Directed by Thomas Carter. DVD. Sony Pictures, 2009.

Harrison, Bob, and James Montgomery. *When God Was Black.* Grand Rapids, MI: Zondervan, 1971.

Nicol, Mike. *Mandela: The Authorized Portrait.* Edited by Kate Parkin. Kansas City, KS: Andrews McMeel Publishing, 2006.

Perkins, John. *Let Justice Roll Down.* Ventura, CA: Regal, 2006.

Civil Rights Movement

Abernathy, Ralph David. *And the Walls Came Tumbling Down: An Autobiography.* New York: Harper & Row, 1989.

Carson, Clayborne, ed. *The Autobiography of Martin Luther King, Jr.* New York: Intellectual Properties Management in association with Warner Books, 1998.

Carson, Clayborne, and Kris Shepard, eds. *A Call to Conscience: The Landmark Speeches of Dr. Martin Luther King, Jr.* New York: Hachette Book Group, 2001. Kindle e-book.

Garrow, David J. *Bearing the Cross: Martin Luther King, Jr., and the Southern Christian Leadership Conference.* New York: Vintage Books, 1988.

In Remembrance of Martin. Directed by Kell Kearns. DVD. PBS Documentary. Paramount Home Entertainment, 1986.

King, Jr., Martin Luther. *The Trumpet of Conscience.* Boston, MA: Beacon Press, 2010.

King, Jr., Martin Luther. *Where Do We Go from Here: Chaos or Community?* Boston, MA: Beacon Press, 1968.

King, Jr., Martin Luther. *Why We Can't Wait.* Boston, MA: Beacon Press, 1964.

Marsh, Charles. *The Beloved Community: How Faith Shapes Social Justice from the Civil Rights Movement to Today.* New York: Basic Books, 2006.

Diversity, Ethnicity, and Race

Banton, Michael. *Racial Theories.* 2nd ed. Cambridge, UK: Cambridge University Press, 1998.

Duke Divinity School. "Joel Perez: God Intended There to Be Color." *Faith and Leadership: An Online Magazine of Leadership Education at Duke Divinity School, Duke University,* 2012. http://www.faithandleadership.com/multimedia/joel-perez-god-intended-there-be-color (accessed August 1, 2012).

Woodley, Randy. *Living in Color: Embracing God's Passion for Ethnic Diversity.* Downers Grove, IL: IVP Books, 2004.

Race and British-American History

Amazing Grace. Directed by Michael Apted. DVD. Twentieth Century Fox, 2006.

Amistad. Directed by Steven Spielberg. DVD. DreamWorks Pictures, 1999.

Bonner, William L. *Black History from a Christian, Scriptural, and Achievement Perspective.* New York: The Church of Our Lord Jesus Christ of the Apostolic Faith, 2009.

Brunt, Deborah. *We Confess! The Civil War, the South, and the Church.* Olive Branch, MS: Key Truths, Open Gates LLC, 2011. Kindle e-book.

David, Jay, ed. *Growing up Black: From Slave Days to the Present.* New York: Avon Books, 1992.

Federer, William J. *America's God and Country: Encyclopedia of Quotations.* St. Louis, MO: Amerisearch, 2000.

The Help. DVD. DreamWorks Pictures, 2011.

The Role of Pastors and Christians in Civil Government. Directed by David Barton. DVD. Wallbuilders, 2002.

Sheets, Dutch, and William Ford III. *History Makers: Your Prayers Have the Power to Heal the Past and Shape the Future.* Ventura, CA: Regal Books, 2004.

Race and the Church

Barna, George, and Harry R Jackson, Jr. *High-Impact African-American Churches: Leadership Concepts from Some of Today's Most Effective Churches.* Ventura, CA: Regal Books, 2004.

Breckenridge, James, and Lillian Breckenridge. *What Color Is Your God? Multicultural Education in the Church.* Grand Rapids, MI: Baker Books, 1998.

Colson, Charles W., and Harold Fickett. *The Faith Given Once, for All: What Christians Believe, Why They Believe It, and Why It Matters.* Grand Rapids, MI: Zondervan, 2008.

Colson, Charles W, and Nancy Pearcey. *How Now Shall We Live?* Wheaton, IL: Tyndale House Publishers, 1999.

Colson, Charles W, and Ellen Santilli Vaughn. *Being the Body: A New Call for the Church to Be Light in the Darkness.* Nashville, TN: W Publishing Group, 2003.

Cordeiro, Wayne. *Doing Church as a Team: The Miracle of Teamwork and How It Transforms Churches.* Ventura, CA: Regal Books, 2004.

DeYoung, Curtiss Paul, Michael O. Emerson, George Yancey, and Karen Chai Kim. *United by Faith: The Multiracial Congregation as an Answer to the Problem of Race.* Oxford, NY: Oxford University Press, 2003. Kindle e-book.

Heflick, John. "A Cornerstone Bridges the Racial Divide." *Connection: The Magazine of Columbia International University,* Spring 2010.

Keener, Craig S., and Glenn Usry. *Defending Black Faith: Answers to Tough Questions About African-American Christianity.* Downers Grove, IL: InterVarsity Press, 1997.

Lincoln, Charles E., and Lawrence H. Mamiya. *The Black Church in the African American Experience*. Durham, NC: Duke University Press, 1990.

Lo, Jim. *Intentional Diversity: Creating Cross-Cultural Ministry Relationships in Your Church*. Indianapolis, IN: Wesleyan Publishing House, 2002.

Lovett, Leonard. *Kingdom Beyond Color: Re-Examining the Phenomenon of Racism*. N.p. Xlibris, 2009.

Marti, Gerardo. *A Mosaic of Believers: Diversity and Innovation in a Multiethnic Church*. Bloomington, IN: Indiana University Press, 2005.

Pocock, Michael, and Joseph Henriques. *Cultural Change and Your Church: Helping Your Church Thrive in a Diverse Society*. Grand Rapids, MI: Baker Books, 2002.

Promise Keepers. "PK History." Promise Keepers. http://www.promisekeepers.org/about/pk-history (accessed March 30, 2013).

Promise Keepers. "The Seven Promises of a Promise Keeper." Promise Keepers. http://www.promisekeepers.org/about/7-promises (accessed March 30, 2013).

Sernett, Milton C, ed. *African American Religious History: A Documentary Witness*. 2nd ed. Durham: Duke University Press, 1999.

Strang, Steve. "What the Pentecostal Voice Can Do." *Charisma*, April 2013.

Strang, Steve, and Harry R. Jackson, Jr. "The Church's Response to Racism." *Charisma*, June 2012.

Tisby, Jemar. *The Color of Compromise: The Truth about the American Church's complicity in Racism*. Grand Rapids, MI: Zondervan, 2019.

Usry, Glenn, and Craig S Keener. *Black Man's Religion: Can Christianity Be Afrocentric?* Downers Grove, IL: InterVarsity Press, 1996.

Williams, Scott. *Church Diversity: Sunday the Most Segregated Day of the Week*. Green Forest, AR: New Leaf Press, 2011.

Wooten, Willie F. *Breaking the Curse off Black America*. Richton Park, IL: Lumen-Us, 2005.

Yancey, George. "An Examination of the Effects of Residential and Church Integration on the Attitudes of Whites." *Sociological Perspectives* 42, no. 2 (Summer 1999): 279–304.

Van Biema, David. "Can Megachurches Bridge the Racial Divide?" *Time Magazine (Online Edition)*, January 11, 2010. http://www.time.com/time/magazine/article/0,9171,1950943,00.ht ml (accessed March 1, 2013).

Van Yperen, Jim. *Making Peace: A Guide to Overcoming Church Conflict*. Chicago, Ill: Moody Press, 2002. Kindle e-book.

Race and Culture

DiversityInc. "Nine Things Never to Say to a White Colleague." DiversityInc, http://www.diversityinc.com/things-not-to-say/9-things-never-to-say-to-white-colleagues/ (accessed February 23, 2013).

DiversityInc. "Ten Things Never to Say to a Black Co-worker." DiversityInc, http://www.diversityinc.com/things-not-to-say/10-things-never-to-say-to-a-black-coworker/ (accessed February 23, 2013).

Elmer, Duane. *Cross-Cultural Conflict: Building Relationships for Effective Ministry*. Downers Grove, IL: InterVarsity Press, 1993.

Ireland, David. *What Color Is Your God? A New Approach to Developing a Multicultural Lifestyle*. Verona, NJ: Impact Pub. House, 2000.

Lane, Patty. *A Beginner's Guide to Crossing Cultures: Making Friends in a Multicultural World*. Downers Grove, IL: InterVarsity Press, 2002.

Norman, Jim, Adriene Bruce, and Michelle Lee. "'You Must Have Voted for Obama': Five Things Never to Say to Blacks." DiversityInc. http://www.diversityinc.com/things-not-to-say/you-must-have-voted-for-obama-5-things-never-to-say-to-blacks/ (accessed February 23, 2013).

Saxe, Godfrey. "The Blind Men and the Elephant." In *The Best Loved Poems of the American People*, edited by Hazel Fellman, 521–22. Garden City, NY: Garden City Books, 1936.

Race and Pentecostal History

A House No Longer Divided. Directed by Darrin J. Rodgers. DVD. Flower Pentecostal Heritage Center, Springfield, MO, 2009.

Alexander, Estrelda. *Black Fire: One Hundred Years of African American Pentecostalism*. Downers Grove, IL: IVP Academic, 2011. Kindle e-book.

Assemblies of God. "Minutes of the 1989 General Council." N.p., n.d.

Blumhofer, Edith. "Revisiting Azusa Street: A Centennial Retrospect." *International Bulletin of Missionary Research* 30, no. 2 (April 1, 2006): 59–64.

Clemmons, Ithiel, Leonard Lovett, Cecil M. Robeck, Jr., and Harold D. Hunter. "Racial Reconciliation Manifesto." *Reconciliation: The Official Journal of the Pentecostal/Charismatic Churches of North America (PCCNA)*, no. 1 (Summer 1998): 17.

Hunter, Harold D. "An Interview with Bishop Gilbert E. Patterson." *Reconciliation: The Official Journal of the Pentecostal/Charismatic Churches of North America (PCCNA)*, no. 1 (Summer 1998): 6–7.

Hunter, Harold D. "Reconciliation - Pentecostal Style." *Reconciliation: The Official Journal of the Pentecostal/Charismatic Churches of North America (PCCNA)*, no. 1 (Summer 1998): 3.

Klaus, Bryon D., ed. *We've Come This Far: Reflections on the Pentecostal Tradition and Racial Reconciliation*. Springfield, MO: Assemblies of God Theological Seminary, 2007.

Robeck, Jr., Cecil M. "Azusa Street Revival." In *The New International Dictionary of Pentecostal and Charismatic Movements*. Rev. ed., edited by Stanley M. Burgess, 344–50. Grand Rapids, MI: Zondervan, 2002.

Roberts, Terry. "Pentecostalism's Greatest Test Could Be Her Finest Hour." *Encounter: Journal for Pentecostal Ministry* 7 (Summer 2010).

http://www.agts.edu/encounter/articles/2010summer/roberts.htm
(accessed April 2, 2013).

Rodgers, Darrin J. "The Assemblies of God and the Long Journey toward
Racial Reconciliation." *Assemblies of God Heritage* 28 (2008): 50–59.

Sanders, Cheryl Jeanne. *Saints in Exile: The Holiness-Pentecostal Experience in
African American Religion and Culture*. New York: Oxford University
Press, 1996.

Synan, Vinson. "Memphis 1994: Miracle and Mandate." *Reconciliation: The
Official Journal of the Pentecostal/Charismatic Churches of North America
(PCCNA)*, no. 1 (Summer 1998): 14–18.

Race, Politics, and Social Justice

Carson, Ben. *America the Beautiful: Rediscovering What Made This Nation Great*.
Grand Rapids, MI: Zondervan, 2012.

Cosby, Bill, and Alvin F Poussaint. *Come on, People: On the Path from Victims to
Victors*. Nashville, TN: Thomas Nelson, 2007.

DeYoung, Curtiss Paul . *Living Faith: How Faith Inspires Social Justice*.
Minneapolis, MN: Fortress Press, 2007. Kindle e-book.

Jackson, Jr, Harry R. *The Truth in Black & White*. Lake Mary, FL: FrontLine,
2008.

Jackson, Jr, Harry R, and Brian Azhnd. "Practically Political: Can Christians
Save the Mess that is Today's American Political Scene?" *Charisma*,
(October 2010): 39–42.

Jackson, Jr, Harry R, and Tony Perkins. *Personal Faith, Public Policy*. Lake
Mary, FL: FrontLine, 2008.

Justice at the Gate. *Democrats and Republicans in their Own Words*. San Antonio,
TX: Justice at the Gate, n.d.

King, Alveda C. "A Covenant with Life." *The Black Republican*, Fall 2008.

Liberty and Justice for All. Directed by Alice Patterson. DVD. Justice at the
Gate, 2003.

Marsh, Charles, and John M. Perkins. *Welcoming Justice: God's Movement toward Beloved Community*. Resources for Reconciliation. Downers Grove, IL: InterVarsity Press, 2009. Kindle e-book.

McKinney, George D. "A God of Justice." *Reconciliation: The Official Journal of the Pentecostal/Charismatic Churches of North America (PCCNA)*, no. 1 (Summer 1998): 4–5.

National Press Club. "Black Clergy Group Opposes Pres. Obama on Gay Marriage." National Press Club. C-SPAN. http://www.c-span.org/Events/Black-Clergy-Group-Opposes-Pres-Obama-on-Gay-Marriage/10737432751/ (accessed September 3, 2012).

Parker, Star. *Uncle Sam's Plantation: How Big Government Enslaves America's Poor and What We Can Do About It*. Nashville, TN: WND BOOKS, 2003.

Patterson, Alice. *Bridging the Racial and Political Divide: How Godly Politics Can Transform a Nation*. San Jose, CA: Transformational Publications, 2010.

Payne, Ruby K. *A Framework for Understanding Poverty*. 4th rev. ed. Highlands, Tex: Aha! Process, 2005.

Runaway Slave: A New Underground Railroad. DVD. Ground Floor, LLC, 2012.

Schmidt, Alvin J. *Under the Influence: How Christianity Transformed Civilization*. Grand Rapids, MI: Zondervan, 2001.

Schoen, Douglas E. *Hopelessly Divided: The New Crisis in American Politics and What It Means for 2012 and Beyond*. Lanham, MD: Rowman & Littlefield Publishers, 2012. Kindle e-book.

Wallis, Jim. *God's Politics: Why the Right Gets It Wrong and the Left Doesn't Get It*. San Francisco: HarperSanFrancisco, 2005.

Racialization (Racial Disparity)

Alexander, Michelle. *The New Jim Crow: Mass Incarceration in the Age of Colorblindness*. New York, NY: The New Press, 2012. Kindle e-book.

Emerson, Michael O, and Christian Smith. *Divided by Faith: Evangelical Religion and the Problem of Race in America*. Oxford; New York: Oxford University Press, 2000.

Reconciliation

Anderson, David A., and Brent Zuercher. *Letters across the Divide: Two Friends Explore Racism, Friendship, and Faith.* Grand Rapids, MI: Baker Books, 2001.

Colby, Tanner. *Some of My Best Friends are Black: The Strange Story of Integration in America.* New York: Viking, 2012. Kindle e-book.

Dawson, John. *Healing America's Wounds.* Ventura, CA: Regal Books, 1994.

DeYoung, Curtiss Paul. *Coming Together in the 21st Century: The Bible's Message in an Age of Diversity.* Valley Forge, PA: Judson Press, 2009.

DeYoung, Curtiss Paul. *Reconciliation: Our Greatest Challenge—Our Only Hope.* Valley Forge, PA: Judson Press, 1997.

Duke Divinity School. "Pumla Gobodo-Madikizela: Forgiveness is Possible." *Faith and Leadership: An Online Magazine of Leadership Education at Duke Divinity School, Duke University,* 2012. http://www.faithandleadership.com/multimedia/pumla-gobodo-madikizela-forgiveness possible?utm_source=newsletter&utm_medium=headline&utm_campaign=FL_topstory (accessed August 1, 2012).

Eidelson, Roy J., and Judy I. Eidelson. "Dangerous Beliefs: Five Beliefs that Propel Groups toward Conflict." *American Psychologist* 58, no. 3 (March 2003): 182–192.

Gobodo-Madikizela, Pumla. *A Human Being Died That Night: A South African Story of Forgiveness.* Boston: Houghton Mifflin, 2003.

Johnson, Melvin L. *Overcoming Racism... through the Gospel.* Longwood, FL: Xulon Press, 2007.

Katongole, Emmanuel, and Chris Rice. *Reconciling All Things: A Christian Vision for Justice, Peace and Healing.* Downers Grove, IL: IVP Books, 2008.

Perkins, Spencer, and Chris Rice. *More Than Equals: Racial Healing for the Sake of the Gospel.* Downers Grove, IL: InterVarsity Press, 2000.

Strang, Steve. "Hope in Sanford: The Untold Story." *Charisma,* June 2012.

The Second Chance. Directed by Steve Taylor. DVD. Sony Pictures, 2006.

Tutu, Desmond. *No Future without Forgiveness.* New York: Doubleday, 2000.

Unconditional. Directed by Brent McCorkle. Provident Films, 2012.

Wells, Samuel, and Marcia A Owen. *Living without Enemies: Being Present in the Midst of Violence.* Downers Grove, IL: IVP Books, 2011. Kindle e-book.

Yoars, Marcus. "Can't We All Just Move On?" *Charisma,* June 2012.

Yoars, Marcus. "Ten Revolutions for the New Year." *Charisma,* January 2013.

ABOUT THE AUTHOR

For 32 years, Dr. Terrell (Terry) Roberts and his wife, Sandra, have served as the founding pastors of Trinity Church in Columbia, South Carolina. As a multi-racial congregation, Trinity Church is something of an anomaly in the heart of the Deep South. Terry is a product of the Jim Crow South, and as a young man, he accepted its racial prejudice and injustice as the norm. Fellowship with African Americans over many years opened his eyes to the beauty and power of ethnic diversity in the local church. Today, he is an advocate, not just for reconciliation, but for authentic *koinonia* (fellowship) across racial lines.

Terry holds a B.A. in Ministry from Southeastern University, a Master of Arts in Bible from Columbia International University, and a Doctor of Ministry in Church Leadership from the Assemblies of God Theological Seminary. His doctoral dissertation focused on racial relations within a multi-ethnic church.

Terry is an executive presbyter with the Assemblies of God in South Carolina and the director of their School of Ministry. Additionally, he serves on the Board of Trustees at Southeastern University in Lakeland, Florida, where he is also an adjunct professor.

Early in his life, he experienced the saving grace of Jesus Christ, resulting in a growing and fulfilling relationship with God. Today, Terry's greatest joy is sharing the message of God's love with others.

Terry and Sandra recently celebrated fifty years of marriage and ministry. They have a daughter, son-in-law, and grand-twins.

OTHER BOOKS BY TERRY ROBERTS
(Available on Amazon or by contacting the author)

Journey to Koinonia:
An Interracial Small Group Experience
The companion to *Beyond Reconciliation*, this book
details a six-week interracial small group
experience, and includes materials and a
facilitator's guide

Passing the Baton:
Planning for Pastoral Transition
A concise resource for pastors and churches to
help them navigate the most challenging change a
congregation will ever face—pastoral transition

Five Timeless Truths:
And Why They Still Matter
In this postmodern age when the concept of
absolute truth has faded, there remain five
enduring realities absolutely essential to life
as it was meant to be lived

Made in United States
Orlando, FL
09 March 2022

15561413R00111